IN MY PAST LIFE I WAS CLEOPATRA

In my PAST LIFE I WAS CLEOPATRA

A sceptical believer's journey
through the New Age

AMAL AWAD

murdoch books

Sydney | London

Published in 2021 by Murdoch Books, an imprint of Allen & Unwin

Murdoch Books Australia
83 Alexander Street, Crows Nest NSW 2065
Phone: +61 (0)2 8425 0100
murdochbooks.com.au
info@murdochbooks.com.au

Murdoch Books UK
Ormond House, 26–27 Boswell Street, London WC1N 3JZ
Phone: +44 (0) 20 8785 5995
murdochbooks.co.uk
info@murdochbooks.co.uk

 A catalogue record for this book is available from the National Library of Australia

A catalogue record for this book is available from the British Library

ISBN 978 1 76052 597 2 Australia
ISBN 978 1 91163 295 5 UK

Cover and text design by Alissa Dinallo
Typeset by Midland Typesetters, Australia
Printed and bound in Australia by Griffin Press

Please note that some names and identifying details have been changed to protect the privacy of individuals.

The content presented in this book is meant for inspiration and informational purposes only. The author and publisher claim no responsibility to any person or entity for any liability, loss, or damage caused or alleged to be caused directly or indirectly as a result of the use, application, or interpretation of the material in this book.

10 9 8 7 6 5 4 3 2 1

 The paper in this book is FSC® certified.
FSC® promotes environmentally responsible, socially beneficial and economically viable management of the world's forests.

To the weavers, wanderers and wise ones in my life,
and those who have come before me

To the seekers

Look at this life — all mystery and magic.

Harry Houdini

CONTENTS

PREFACE

I was raised in a religious household, so belief and practice have been formative staples in my life from a young age. As an Arab, I grew up with a keen awareness of the way the muddy remnants of Turkish coffee can help you to divine your future. As a Muslim, I understood that there were unseen forces at play in my life, and things like superstition, fatalism and mysterious jinn were more real to me than any Hollywood fantasy. But over the years, this has shifted and evolved. I now see that many things can be true for people, but what makes all the difference is who is believing it and how that belief plays out in their lives. That is to say, *how* we believe, not simply what we accept as true, tends to say a lot about who we are and how we see the world.

Because of this, my journey as a spiritual seeker has developed numerous shades of meaning. From religious devotion to New Age love and light, I have tried a *lot*. As life demonstrates daily, something that works for one person might be meaningless to another. So I try to keep an open mind and make sense of things, rather than define a single truth.

For me, it has always been about finding a way to *be* in the world with some level of comfort and ease. But while I have an open mind, I have no qualms erecting boundaries where I think the New Age is problematic. This discernment is crucial; and it's what makes me a believer who is also sceptical. I see a lot of things as true or possible, but I am more curious than fervent. Importantly, I don't think everything requires proof. I am rarely definitive about anything but what I feel and how my life changes as a result of what I call 'inner work'. As a psychic healer named Jasmine Hawkins once told me, I'm 'a believer who wants to believe'. (Besides, science takes care of a lot of the dangerous hooey you will find in some fields of Mind, Body, Spirit.)

And you see, this is exactly *why* I'm the right person to take you on this journey. As someone who was raised to believe in God and the supernatural, and as someone who has never stopped seeking (and hopefully never will), I've been the guinea pig; I've negotiated belief and faith, landed hard on my butt more than once, but also expanded my mind enough to take in new ways of looking at the world. I am sceptical of a lot of things, just not everything, and that is simply because I don't believe everything demands proof. I also believe wholeheartedly in our right to difference, to follow an authentic and individual path. You do you and all that, with the obvious proviso that your ideas, beliefs or practices should not be hurting others or affecting their free will. Nothing criminal, cruel or harmful.

As I was nearing completion of this book, the world seemed to implode. A weary Australia had just come off a summer of devastating bushfires that decimated nature, homes and wildlife. Soon after, the globe was hit by the COVID-19 pandemic. Along with the climate crisis and economic uncertainty, it's no exaggeration to say that I was writing this during a challenging period in our history.

At times like these, spiritual fulfilment can seem like a luxury, or a 'non-essential item'. But for me, the opposite is true: your inner world will crucially help to sustain you during any crisis. It is during periods of struggle that we most need to maintain our mental and physical wellbeing, as well as do whatever we can to preserve and nurture meaningful connection — to our fellow humans, to ourselves, and to the world. This is the spirit in which this book is intended, and with which I explore belief and the New Age.

The reality is, we all benefit from having a toolkit in life, now more than ever. My many years of seeking have helped me to create mine — and I hope this book helps you to create yours. Find what soothes your soul, and try to bring that energy into the world.

We're all in this together.

INTRODUCTION

I am an inquisitive explorer, I tell myself as I enter the Heart Space Centre in an industrial suburb a stretch too far from home. It's the type of area you come to for a set of new tyres or super cheap electronics. But on this rain-soaked Sydney evening, I have come to connect to my dragon.

At the Heart Space Centre (not its real name, but it could be), a staircase leads you into a room that could very well double for a physiotherapy clinic, but instead of a waiting area, foam rollers and foldable massage tables, there are bookshelves lined with oracle decks, crystals, wands and New Age books — everything from the fall of Atlantis to the way we self-sabotage in our daily lives.

I have been to this particular den of Zen before and it's a welcoming space. The women who run it are down-to-earth. They sit high on the 'woo woo' scale, sure, but they don't lavishly declare it. They wear normal clothes, the kind you buy from Zara, and while they run workshops and accommodate spiritual facilitators, they are not out to convince you of any one thing. You can visit the centre for things like reiki, chakra balancing techniques, soul healings and your garden-variety psychic readings. They offer workshops aplenty, and the beaming smiles are free.

In the middle of the room is a large altar assembled for the session. There are rose-coloured metal pyramids, crystals, a bronze Tibetan singing bowl for sound healing and . . . blocks of chocolate. The altar has been 'reikied', which means the space has been infused with big chunks of universal love, as has the chocolate (making it not just delicious but a spiritual pick-me-up).

I suppose you could argue that there's something here for everyone, but not just anyone comes here. Every New Age place I have visited has a distinct vibe. It attracts a certain group of people and, while I think well of the women running the Heart Space Centre, I feel out of place here tonight, at this dragon connection workshop. It's not the reikied chocolate or pyramids, or that I don't have anything in common with the others here (who are, incidentally, all women) — it's more that they're 'true believers'.

You see, I'm what I like to call a 'sceptical believer'. Now, I know what you're thinking: how can you be both a sceptic *and* a believer? Stop wasting our time, fence-sitter! But my brand of scepticism is not about cynicism or distrust; it's about discernment. The creative writer in me wants to explore everything that belief has to offer, but never far behind is the questioning journalist, who keeps me from falling for any old hokum.

And this is what has brought me here: curiosity, and a desire to learn. I'm here to see what it's all about; what is meant by 'dragon energy' (before Kanye West ruined it for us all).

I'm still second-guessing myself as I take a seat among the women of the group, most of whom seem pretty friendly, though there are others who are slightly stand-offish. I remember how competitive New Age types can be ('I'll raise your psychic ability with my near-death experience at the age of ten!').

Before leading us into a journey to connect to our dragon, Chanel (not her real name, but it could be) matter-of-factly explains how dragons are here to help us on earth. Apparently, I can call on my dragon to help me if I'm in need; like when I'm stuck in traffic, or feeling lost, or for any other life issues that require a sweeping out of old, stagnant energy. And no two dragons are the same: there are earth dragons, water dragons, ones that fly (air) and ones that set things on fire (self-explanatory). Some dragons encompass more than one element.

All of this is great for my creative brain; plump fodder for my imagination and valuable information for a lover of all things mystical and supernatural. But I'm feeling embarrassed, because I'm not a true believer. And I know the competition may get fierce, as we out-dragon each other.

In a meditative state, we are led by Chanel, and I am pleasantly transported to an earthy, lush place where there is grass of a lovely soft green and water as blue as the sky. And because I am being guided, I'm using my imagination to create a story. Beyond the mountains, a dragon comes into view; she is my dragon. She finds me on the grass and I try to figure out how she looks. I decide that she is white, but I know that a part of me is just picturing Falkor, the Luckdragon companion of the hero Atreyu in

The Neverending Story. So it's difficult to trust it when I try to make her more 'real'. I decide that she is more feminine and dragon-like than Falkor, who was too large, and, well, male. She flew to me so she is obviously an air dragon. And when our instructor tells us to find out our dragon's name, the name Cleo pops up in my mind's eye.

My dragon's name is Cleo.

I share my dragon findings with the group following the meditation, but I lack the enthusiasm and confidence of my fellow travellers. I'm not a gun like the woman a few seats down who has always been a friend to dragons and struggled because an entire horde of them flanked her during the meditation.

I'm reminded of another odd group meditation I once attended, where we journeyed to Lemuria, the 'first civilisation', followed by a quick stop in Atlantis. When you 'journey' to a place in meditation, you generally experience that world as you, no matter how unreal the realm you're visiting. No matter how you see yourself, such meditation is meant to benefit through insight it affords you about your actual life.

The competition that night was far fiercer than the workshop with the dragons. One woman hadn't just found her past-life Lemurian self, she was downloading a new healing 'modality' (the word New Agers use to describe a method of healing). Symbols everywhere. Even our hosts looked taken aback, a slight question in their expressions. But she waved them away. 'Still downloading,' she said, and the room hushed in reverence.

Following the dragon-seeking meditation, and not for

the first time, I wonder at the human capacity to conjure so many techniques and practices to treat simple issues.

From psychics and mediums to spirit guides and past lives, the New Age taps into essential parts of our lives — our physical and mental wellbeing, how we see ourselves, how we take on the world and, in general, how we live. In all of this, there are people searching for something more: an experience of the divine.

Fantastical transformation

While dragons feature heavily in mythology and modern fantasy literature, there are New Agers who genuinely believe in their existence, along with unicorns and faeries. It may be that they are connecting to what they perceive as the 'energies' of these beings, but others seem more literal in their understanding of mythological entities. One well-known New Age writer, Diana Cooper, believes we're in an age of ascension and that the earth is entering into a period of dragon energy. She unapologetically meditates with unicorns and dragons, documenting them in the way of a fervent anthropologist on a newly discovered island.

Like all things New Age, it's not necessarily about the idea (dragons, unicorns, your higher self), but the metaphor (transformation). The dragon meditation, or any kind of activity that draws on mythology or fantasy, can be effective if it's a transformative experience. Most beliefs, ideas and practices are packed with meaning, lessons for the modern age and for the lost soul. And while the New Age involves innovation, much of it is lifted liberally from Shamanic traditions, indigenous mythologies and the world's major religions. In other words, it massages existing ideas and beliefs, and is not new.

Which goes some way to explain why it's difficult to decipher where more traditional spirituality and religious practice begin and New Age ends.

WHAT IS 'NEW AGE'?

The term 'New Age' refers to a mystical approach to exploring and practising various traditions and beliefs. There is debate about when and where the term originated, but it came to prominence with the Harmonic Convergence in 1987 (an event New Agers considered a synchronised global meditation and a return to harmony). New Age thinking can be applied to any set of attitudes, from business to environmentalism, but most of us think of it primarily in relation to the Mind, Body, Spirit (MBS) industries. While there is some overlap between the three branches of MBS, they can broadly be defined as follows:

MIND: Self-help, focusing on mental wellbeing, motivation, peace of mind and positive thinking.

BODY: Physical wellness — everything from gym workouts to yoga, healthy eating, essential oils and super foods.

SPIRIT (sometimes called 'Soul'): Traditional and newer forms of spirituality and religion.

New Agers have a particular affinity with the category of Spirit, though they often dabble in all three branches of MBS.

Today, New Age industries are a free-for-all marketplace of ideas with something for everyone. Are you looking for a goddess archetype? An experience of transcendence? To discover the Buddha within? Advice on how to win at life? A diet that works best combined with crystal massages? (It could happen.) It's a world that is swelling into unmanageable proportions, with its own language, including an actual light language (channelled cosmic communication), hierarchies with priestesses and goddess circles, special souls who identify as lightworkers, earth angels, star children and so on. Whatever your need or desire, the New Age has got you covered.

This is not to say every person interested in the New Age accepts all of it. I'm sure a lot of them are just like me, interested in aspects, alert and open to how something can work as a healing or wellbeing measure, rather than why.

Meanwhile, the sense of self-importance in New Age circles can be a hoot. I don't think anyone has more accurately satirised the self-importance of some New Age followers than JP Sears, aka Ultra Spiritual, whose wildly popular 'Awaken With JP' Youtube videos (such as 'How to take yoga photos for Instagram') have amassed millions of views. It's worth noting that he mocks an industry he seems well-versed in, so I would wager that — like me — he has some investment in it. When he recently shared a non-ironic Facebook post about attending a Tony Robbins seminar, this seemed to confirm it.

The beauty of the New Age is that it is built to cater to our differences, which is arguably both its strength and its problem. There is so much on offer that you can happily focus on the things you like. You can dip in and out of it, or you can make it a way of life. You will see people who are simply curious or investigating something new, and others who consider it their calling to be a healer or save the world. It is often transformative, and never boring.

SO, WHAT IS THIS BOOK YOU'RE ABOUT TO READ?

A memoir, a critique or a guide? The answer is: all of the above. It is a tour through the New Age world, down avenues of personal experience, with additional insight from practitioners and experts in various fields. As such, the book starts with an overview of what I call 'the world of woo woo', followed by a personal journey through religious faith, self-help and scepticism, and a variety of New Age modalities — from witchcraft and magic, to divination and crystals.

As a sceptical believer, it's not my intention to skewer the industry or dissolve beliefs; indeed, I want to challenge the idea that all spiritual pursuit is hokum, pseudoscience, or blind, misplaced faith. From my own experience, I think there is something to it all, and it's meant to be felt and experienced. There is also plenty of scientific research to bind New Age spirituality with improved wellbeing — such that the benefits of meditation and the subset of 'mindfulness' are now part of everyday speak, even in the workplace. But the problems start when New Age practices stop being a free pursuit of faith and veer into money-making greed, are designed to secure power (akin to a cult), or endanger people's health or emotional lives. That last one in particular is where much of the criticism is laid: when 'solutions' without any scientific grounding or proven efficacy are offered to handle or 'cure' illness, past trauma or other afflictions better treated by qualified experts. It's always best to consult a healthcare professional first when it comes to matters of physical and mental health.

But if there is a whole lot of dodgy behaviour and greed in the New Age industries, it's because there's a whole lot of that in humanity as well, and no amount of dragon meditations or transcendent experience is going to change this.

As someone who has, at times, struggled to reconcile scepticism with faith and a desire to believe, I wish to help you explore how you can loosen these chains and find your own spiritual path. There is a lot of good in the world of woo woo — the key is discernment.

When considering this mash-up of beliefs and practices, it's important to appreciate that New Age is a newborn in a world that has, for as long as humans have existed, looked to nature and beyond to make sense of life and our invisible guardians. If you're a seeker like I am, I hope you'll find something in the following pages that speaks to you and will spark your own journey, or strengthen the one you are already on.

CHAPTER ONE

The World of Woo Woo

I'm surrounded by people in the throes of a religious moment. Arms and hands outstretched, eyes closed in a moment of surrender, with all the feels, listening as a singer intones words of reassurance, self-worth and love. In support and leading us all on stage is Sunny Dawn Johnston, who occasionally repeats the lyrics, her hands open in submission and her eyes closed. She's tiny. Leather pants and blonde hair. She's like musical theatre star Kristin Chenoweth, but cooler and more spiritual.

I've made a huge mistake, I decide, wincing with embarrassment because I'm wedged between true believers with glitter stamps on their faces and a clear openness to being healed. I find it excruciating because I grew up in Australia where we're all self-conscious and shy away from public vulnerability. And I'm of Arab heritage, where ditto. Sure,

Australia may have taken the affirmation-drenched baton and ran with it, like most Western countries, but we're not so wholehearted in embracing it.

It crystallises for me how private and guarded I am with my own spirituality and its connection to the New Age; how my scepticism remains an essential thread. I'm unable to limit myself to one way, one truth, and to declare it so openly and easily. I have travelled far for this, so it would be disingenuous for me to suggest that attending a conference called Celebrate Your Life! (CYL) is purely an exercise in sceptical curiosity. And I certainly haven't come to poke fun at the masses who long for a more fulfilling life.

No. I can make fun of a lot of things — including myself and the sometimes outlandish ways in which I seek inner peace, spiritual satisfaction and higher purpose. And it is this desire for peace, satisfaction and purpose that really brings me here. I like to see it all up close, not just in a newsletter in my inbox, or a download from Amazon. I want to see what it's all about, what this pull is towards speakers who claim to have found New Age solutions for their problems.

The mood is palpable. More than 1200 people have converged on this high-end hotel in downtown Phoenix, Arizona, enticed to, well, celebrate their lives! (Note the exclamation mark: this is not for the faint of heart.) There is a slate of big-name keynote speakers — the who's who of the modern New Age realm. James Redfield of *The Celestine Prophecy*, Neale Donald Walsch of *Conversations with God*, the prolific Caroline Myss (a medical intuitive and archetype expert) and Dr Joe Dispenza, whose book

Breaking the Habit of Being Yourself still graces top ten self-help lists years after its publication.

I only know about this at all because I'm subscribed to the newsletter of oracle card expert Colette Baron-Reid, who dispenses weekly prescriptive readings on YouTube to thousands of followers, and also happens to be appearing at CYL. I love her. I have used some of her card decks for years. She's cool, self-deprecating, and has always seemed wise, genuine in trying to steer people towards a more creative approach to their lives. There are more like her, and to me they are the rock stars of the so-called New Age movement.

They are also, it's worth noting, predominantly white speakers addressing a predominantly white audience. I don't think there is anything wrong with that per se; but it tells me that the world we are entering here is a distinctly Western, as opposed to Eastern, expression of spirituality.

For the next few days, delegates will attend talks about everything from the quantum field of infinite possibilities (because science is the language of modern spirituality) to how we can connect to deceased loved ones. We will shop for crystals and oracle decks, and bath bombs with a message that explode to reveal a crystal (it's 'awakening' and an amethyst for me), and have our toes read (a warm experience where a woman named Lourdes tells me that my second toe reveals my life path involves communication).

At the time of the conference, the US is readying itself for the 2018 mid-term elections, which would offer a reading on national satisfaction with then-President Donald Trump's leadership. Despite the infectious positivity, an energy of doom permeates the space. The night before, a politically charged Marianne Williamson, New Age author, activist and spiritual leader, offered the first keynote, despairing at one point that *'he's our president'* with audible disgust. Since then, Williamson has launched, and ended, a presidential campaign. She's not the only woman who threw her hat in the ring, but she's the only one from the world of woo woo.

A CYL regular for fifteen years, Williamson received a hero's welcome following an introduction from the MC who looked like she would implode from excitement. Attendees took snaps of Williamson as she began with a meditation. 'We have been brought here this weekend by divine assignment,' she told us, eventually ending her invocations with an 'amen'.

Williamson's talk focused on the responsibility people hold in life to make the world a better place. Given her audience of New Age devotees, I was taken aback when she scolded the manifestation-focused types who chase desires rather than surrender themselves as a vessel to spirit. She wanted us to know that all things move in the direction of greater life and divine actualisation and enlightenment. Divine intelligence is at work in all things. A tree is programmed to be a tree, and so on.

Her admonishing vibe took me by surprise. At the time, I knew only that Williamson was famous for *A Return to Love*, her book condensing *A Course in Miracles*, a dense work whose author claims was channelled through the holy spirit. Williamson, whom I later discovered was once a preacher, is at home in the New Age space, with her focus on love and service to spirit. She is bold, definitive and her words are steeped in surrender and trust in the divine plan. More than that, there's a sense of obligation and humility that people familiar with religion are likely to recognise.

Maybe this is why her talk jarred in tone for me — I found it less inspirational and more judgemental; identifying a person's vulnerability (wanting things they don't have, feeling inadequate, being adrift in a world that offers spiritual relief in too many ways to follow). The only surrender Williamson seemed interested in was to spirit, who will dictate how you can be of use. Her approach is a strand of the New Age, but also at odds with some of the messages of your garden-variety New Age speaker, where the focus is on self-determination and self-love, empowerment, creating the life you desire.

I left during question time, feeling like I'd just been beaten around the head with a spiritual baton. Others filtered out, as is common when the main talk is done and dusted, but Williamson had the crowd on side for the most part.

I have to concede that she has a point regarding humanity's obsession with manifesting rather than living. In a way, Williamson is pointing out the contradictions of an industry that at once capitalises on the idea of self-achievable bliss while also admonishing those who don't respect divine law and order, especially with regard to the timing of how things unfold in life.

Manifest things and think positively!
But wait, it's all about divine timing, trust and faith.

This is notable also given the emphasis in the New Age on spiritual contracts that supposedly bind us in this life — the idea that an unknowable version of ourselves from another realm or past life made some major life decisions for us before we were set forth from the womb. A confusing proposition for an industry that runs on the fuel of empowerment and creating your own destiny.

This is where I perhaps struggle the most in the New Age space: its vastness and its ambition to pinpoint truth. I worry about the potential harm that can occur in telling a vulnerable person that they signed up for the challenges they're going through before they were birthed into this world.

It was refreshing to read a post by psychic reader Nicole Cody on her blog *Cauldrons and Cupcakes*, which seemed to reject the notion that life is dictated by karma or soul contracts, or that the props of the New Age hold the power you lack. Like Cody, many will reject this limiting idea that you somehow signed up for a challenging life in order to learn lessons.

The next morning, before the singing and Sunny Dawn Johnston, I encountered delegates in the lift gushing about Williamson's keynote. The sort of effusive comments you would expect from diehard fans. Descriptors like 'amazing' and 'loved her'. I remembered how much she sounded like a preacher. I wondered if she was melding aspects of the Christian faith into the New Age.

'Is she Christian?' I queried, I thought innocently enough, only to be met with stony silence. They seemed taken aback. All except one woman, who chatted with me as we made our way to breakfast.

I asked her about the reaction in the elevator and she shrugged. She suggested that Williamson might have offended, even triggered, people in the audience as well. 'I mean, how would you feel if you were a Republican?'

THE 'NEW' AGE?

A few years ago, rumours swirled that Oprah Winfrey would run for president in 2020, following her rousing speech at an awards ceremony (because after Trump, why not another celebrity?). There was a variety of responses, including one from Kurt Andersen, who, in an adapted extract from his book *Fantasyland: How America Went Haywire* for *Slate*, blames Oprah for her part in what he calls 'the irrational, pseudoscientific free for all'. He calls her 'an ecumenical promoter of fantasies', to whom many of the New Age industry's 'best-known prophets and denominational leaders' owe their careers — Deepak Chopra, Marianne Williamson and Eckhart Tolle to name just three.

Andersen may be overstating things, but fair enough on the 'free for all'. If the so-called 'New' Age is a mosh pit of ideas, beliefs and traditions, can we pinpoint where it all began?

Human history is a storied one, with its sheer cornucopia of beliefs and rituals. We are a practical lot, and even if you're not a believer, fervent or otherwise, you believe in something, or at least carry a bunch of ideas around all day. This is our humanity at work; we need to have something to work towards, to flesh out our lives, to feel like there is more to our everyday existence than survival. We have this luxury nowadays, to deep dive into ourselves, to correspond with our souls and 'higher selves', to be philosophical and grow our perspectives on invisible realms.

Humans' fascination with the unseen and unknowable continues even when we consider ourselves smarter and more technologically advanced than ever before. In the New Age, we remain firmly connected to our ancestry, beholden to the experiences and teachings of those who have come before us.

If we were to trace our connection to the unseen, it would begin with animism, the belief that the world is animated by spirits, which is still believed by many today. Animism is prehistoric, arguably the world's oldest religion, with variations in its practice over time, such as Shinto. Shamanism followed, also prehistoric, dating back to Paleolithic cultures (30,000 years ago), and coming out of Siberia. Then came the gods and goddesses, the rise of various monotheistic Abrahamic faiths (Judaism, Christianity and Islam), and spiritual offshoots like Sufism or Kabbalah. We've had enlightenment and spiritual pursuit (Taoism, Buddhism and the like). We've seen spiritualism and pantheism, which links to ideas of 'oneness' with its belief that we *are* God, along with a whole range of other beliefs and practices. (This is a crude condensation of human history. For a thorough and yet somehow remarkably concise summary of humanity's conception of God and variations on divine interaction, I recommend reading Reza Aslan's *God*. In it, Aslan takes you on an informative tour of how we believe and why (often, it can be motivated by practical reasons and a desire for power).)

All of this has fed into the New Age, which *The Encyclopedia of Crystals, Herbs, & New Age Elements* dates back to the 1970s, when counterculture spirituality was groovy, man. And just like many of the time-honoured traditions laid out above, the New Age has proved equally tenacious.

Reporting for *The Guardian* in 2018, Emma Featherstone discussed a 'revival of new age spirituality', with reference to rising interest in witchcraft. It's not unusual to see publications for twenty- and thirty-somethings covering New Age practices and sacred traditions revised for a modern audience. Astrology has long been a staple in popular culture and media, but now we're seeing a resurgence in tarot cards and oracular practice, too. Fashion and beauty has also seen value in the New Age. Featherstone notes a Dior collection that features images from a tarot deck, and beauty products that have gemstones and crystals in them. Jewellery brands are big on using stones and New Age imagery (dreamcatcher pendants and so on), and popular crystal jeweller Swarovski launched a collection that centres tarot and magic. Evil eyes, across all of these things, are par for the course. I've even seen a large pool float in the shape of a blue eye.

There are numerous articles around the rise or revival of witchcraft, linking it to astrology. Tarot cards now also occupy the realm of artists and storytellers, with a recent initiative of 50 artists around the world diversifying the tarot in an exhibition and complementary card deck called 'What Does Our Future Hold?'. And tattoo artists make good coin illustrating New Age-inspired imagery (feathers, sacred geometry and so on).

Elsewhere, you can see the normalisation of traditions so that they are fun and accessible. For example, one mainstream Australian publication that is half-sensationalist storytelling, half-puzzles, instructed readers on how to make their own 'faery door'. Psychics have dedicated pages in women's magazines. There are innumerable hotlines, live TV readings with famous psychics and mediums, and pop-culture offerings that continue to plumb the depths of the supernatural.

But in a way, nothing is truly being revived. It's simply flourishing in an online-supported world, where people in the New Age space can more easily attract a global following, and cross-culturally send out their message. YouTube and other social media portals have made way for internet celebrities, the ones who have forged careers outside of the traditional content publishing structures. One 'practical witch' on YouTube has more than 300,000 followers. Views on her videos are in the tens of thousands.

The truth about humanity is that we require belief, even if it's in the rejection of the idea of something greater than ourselves. And it has never been easier to find things that can sate our thirst for meaning.

In an article for Intelligencer in *New York* magazine, politically conservative writer Andrew Sullivan considers 'America's New Religions', in which the practising Roman Catholic argues that everyone has a religion, by which he means: 'a practice not a theory' that goes back 'to some transcendent value, undying "Truth" or God (or gods)'. And this means that even atheists have a form of religion, in the sense that they hold an absolute belief, and values by which to live. Sullivan makes a pertinent point about modern practices. He has 'brilliant' atheist friends like Bob Wright and Sam Harris, who can see the value of Buddhism (a religion that, ingeniously, does not have a god, Sullivan adds), and who practise Vipassana meditation and mindfulness. It's interesting to note that even those most fervent unbelievers can find value in the one spiritual thing that works for them.

I can't disagree with Sullivan's observation about belief. It carries and sustains us, and reveals much about how we see ourselves or our stage of life. And I find it interesting that one can be spiritual but atheist. Increasingly, we are seeing greater exploration of how this works. Alain de Botton, in *Religion for Atheists*, searches for the connectivity between truth and fantasy in religion; and in her book *For Small Creatures Such as We*, Sasha Sagan (the daughter of famous astronomer and scientist Carl Sagan) extols the value of ritual when you are without a traditional jumping-off point, such as a religious holiday.

Spiritual pursuit is not confined to witchcraft and mountain-top meditators, but it involves a desire to connect to unknown or invisible beings — deities, spirits, elementals perhaps. The spiritual seeker wants communion with divine forces, but also to achieve peace, and to be gazing inward, rather than be focused on the external world.

If the New Age is a world concerned with healing and transformation, what are we becoming once we feel healed and transformed? Friends and I have joked in the past about how dealing with one problem seems to unravel a fresh one. It can seem like a never-ending journey. But I have a better grasp on this now: we are constantly evolving, something my Vedic meditation practice (which I discuss more fully in Chapter Eight) has helped me to understand. It's not a search or a quest with an 'end point', an idea that perhaps our love of stories has built in our minds.

What if all of this practice and soul-seeking is not about obliterating problems but changing the way they play out in our minds and lives? What if having a more general sense of peace means we are less stressed, more purposeful and led by connection to things that cannot always be explained? What if, sometimes, the experience of something is all that really matters, rather than our understanding of its mechanics?

But not everything in the New Age sphere is about spiritual fulfilment or even curiosity, or the aesthetics of enlightenment. Increasingly, in its quest for legitimacy, it is also about proof. If modern New Agers aren't celebrating the return of the divine feminine, they are talking about the language of mysticism in scientific terms.

Quantum physics is the current darling of New Age workings — specifically 'the unified field'. I'm not a scientist, and I nearly failed physics in high school, but here goes: there is, instead of both a physical field and virtual field, a single unified field. In both the New Age and some spiritual traditions, this is what is called a field of consciousness. Think of us all — every being and object — as connected, like an ocean. One drop cannot be distinct from another in an ocean. We have no beginning or end.

Dr Joe Dispenza, the wildly popular author of *Breaking the Habit of Being Yourself*, has written extensively on this. His work is heavily tuned in to science, but he also leans towards mysticism (he is a doctor, scientist and a 'modern-day mystic' according to the foreword in his book *Becoming Supernatural*). For example, in his work he speaks of 'tugging on the garment of the divine' in meditation.

Vedic meditation has helped me better understand 'oneness', a concept that permeates most traditions and religions, including Islam. Ibn 'Arabi, a Sufi mystic and scholar (b. 1165), offered poetic and spacious thoughts on unity with God. I suppose it's what Carl Jung called the 'collective unconscious' (one mind all humanity is connected to); or what a lot of New Agers are calling 'the universal consciousness'. In Islam, Muslims speak of *tawhid*, an indivisible oneness with God.

'Consciousness' is an essential entry in New Age vocabulary. You may even detect a rise in 'Christ consciousness', not necessarily from Christians, but from New Age wanderers who dip in and out of religions and spiritual pathways. This taps into an idea of unification of the whole, of oneness with God and all there is. But in a generic way, it refers simply to the collective mind of humanity. Our consciousness; it has shifted over the history of our existence on the planet. Where our consciousness lies will tell us about our evolution, our progress, how we see and behave in the world.

'Consciousness' is a term that will probably make some people cringe. But I don't mind it so much. When people speak of a shift or rise in consciousness, it rings true. It points to the way humanity in general thinks and creates and moves. Consciousness is the #metoo movement; gun debates in the US; youth lobbying and rallying for the environment. There is still plenty to be done. We evolve constantly, but the point is that we *can* evolve. Because if we are not making change, then we are stagnant and not really living at all.

APPRECIATION OR APPROPRIATION?

When you've been an experimenter with New Age-type stuff for a while, you start to connect the dots. Most of the things you will find — courses, books, orations, oracular offerings, healings, meditations and more — plug into universal human angst, anxiety and longing, and draw on various ancient practices, wisdoms or long-held beliefs.

Consider the popularity of oracle decks, which revolve around shamanic principles (invisible spirits existing in the visible world), the occult, divinity, nature and spirituality. Once again, the options are numerous; something for every traveller. While it's not unusual to see indigenous mythologies or figures from Eastern religions and traditions in card decks, I was surprised when I flipped through *The Divine Feminine Oracle* by Meggan Watterson, just one deck that draws on many traditions. Not unlike the goddess decks in the oracle marketplace, this one also brings in the feminine energies often referred to as ascended masters. Where Watterson truly departs from the norm is her inclusion of Muslim women from Islamic history: Rabi'a al-Adawiyya, the Sufi mystic and saint; and a veiled Fatimah, the daughter of the Prophet Muhammed.

In her book *Wellmania*, Brigid Delaney's description of her search for serenity through religion explores the idea of 'spiritual shopping'. She speaks of global journeys that brought her into contact with the world's major religions, but also people who had reinvented them, stripping them 'for parts' to deliver 'something new, modern and strange'.

Global cultures are the make-up of the New Age. Perhaps it's a distillation process of sorts for the restless traveller: we accumulate knowledge, and recognise that older traditions understand human complexity and desire in ways that still tap into the emotional and spiritual experience of being human. The New Age tends to 'innovate' things, but it plays with timeless truths. Just about everything I have encountered over the years, and continue to find, is a reinterpretation of philosophies and belief systems and ideas that have served humans for millennia.

There is no denying that cultural and religious appropriation — or worse, theft — occurs across many industries. You see it often in modern gastronomy: how many Western chefs are experts in another culture's cuisine, or offer a fusion of East and West? It can get political in food, too. There is a difference between being influenced by flavours or food, and claiming them as your own. Do you want the cheap food court version with no nutritional value, or the authentic, nourishing one? Similarly, do you want the bargain-basement pre-packaged crystal kit, or the one you know has been imported honestly and fairly?

A friend recently raised this when she told me that she struggles to do yoga. She feels like it's not her culture, that it's disingenuous to attend classes. I'm not convinced that's true. Yoga was brought to the West by Indian monks (not Gwyneth Paltrow) and embraced heartily in many forms. It is OK to have a Western audience. Experiences don't necessarily belong to one culture. Having said that, I do believe it is inappropriate to disrespectfully traffic in cultural and religious traditions, using them incorrectly or carelessly, or with profit in mind.

The troubling result of blind appropriation or wild embrace without understanding can be found in the public reception of a Japanese woman who has taught people about how decluttering their possessions will change their lives.

Marie Kondo exploded onto the scene with her book, *The Life-Changing Magic of Tidying Up*, and a series on Netflix, which sees the diminutive and softly-spoken Japanese woman enter the homes of American families and instruct them on her KonMari method (including sorting through belongings and only keeping those that 'spark joy', and following a particular folding technique for clothes).

Even though Westerners jumped on Kondo's work, swore by it, decluttered feverishly and drove op-shop workers insane following the Netflix series, they also didn't fully understand it.

Writing for *HuffPost*, Margaret Dilloway thoughtfully tackles this ignorance, with an article headlined 'What White, Western Audiences Don't Understand About Marie Kondo's "Tidying Up"'. Dilloway points to the Shinto roots of Kondo's method. She recalls how her mother, who 'practised a Shinto mindset, stubbornly and daily' at home, guided her to an idea that all creations deserved respect. Her mother would instruct her to clap her hands three times, 'so the kami know you're here'.

Kami are Shinto spirits that exist everywhere, in every being, thing and nature, Dilloway explains, before delving into Shinto animism and its concepts. Dilloway artfully unpacks Shinto ways of life, which see observers treat objects they own as having value rather than as disposable.

Dilloway notes the disparaging comments and memes, criticisms that insulted Japanese culture and mockery that was xenophobic, even from peers who are 'otherwise empathetic and culturally sensitive'. She cites white writer Anakana Schofield who, in an article for *The Guardian*, seems offended by the suggestion to tap on books to 'wake them up'. She indignantly mocks tapping books with 'fairy finger motions', arguing that reading its contents aloud achieves this. Schofield points to the 'woo-woo nonsense territory we are in'.

The New Age may sometimes attract mockery of this sort, but it is also enticing. It looks enlightened and exotic, exciting and mystical. It is otherworldly and expansive, but it borrows freely from non-Anglo cultures. It is based on ideas, beliefs and knowledge that is as old as human civilisation, except it's also modernised, shrink-wrapped and sold to the masses in convenient bite-sized chunks.

The world is increasingly accessible in its globalisation. In Western multicultural societies, it's easy to import exotic and mysterious traditions, otherness that speaks your language. Writing for NITV in Australia, Natalie Cromb lays into the generous pilfering of cultural iconography and sacred objects: the white artist who dons a geisha outfit in a music video; the lingerie model who wears a Native American headdress as she struts down the runway in her underwear. 'Indigenous people are particularly vulnerable to their culture being appropriated by non-Indigenous people and due to their minority status, most often are not listened to by the mainstream populace,' she writes.

Cromb also calls for a better understanding of when appreciation becomes appropriation. 'The difference between appreciation and appropriation comes down to respect.'

It's something I spoke to oracle card expert Colette Baron-Reid about, roughly a year after I saw her at CYL in Phoenix. In recent times, she has faced serious challenges to her overall thinking — a journey that has been important, but also liberating. With more than eleven decks behind her, Colette has applied a new lens to her efforts, revisiting her decks to address the use of Native American imagery following numerous criticisms.

'I'd adopted the kind of hippy New Age attitude that all of it is based in genuine appreciation and desire to show diversity, like many of my contemporaries in this arena,' she told me. Good intentions are fine, but are not enough. Rather than play out a lengthy and ineffective apology, Colette hired two diversity and inclusivity, and anti-racism coaches. She also inspected her own ancestry and spiritual influences.

'Once you start opening your eyes you can't unsee these things . . . Some people refuse this when they're hit with it. But I honestly don't think we can ignore any of it if we want what we say we want — a unified world!'

Colette dived deep to address the situation. 'I faced my own personal biases, looked at how my privilege plays into things, and came to realise how I was participating in a harmful system,' she said. 'I started to make changes, which I will likely be working on for the rest of my life.'

Colette calls herself a student in an ongoing situation. 'But I believe we're all responsible for how we engage the subject of racism and appropriation and why we need to change.'

Colette's publisher, Hay House (founded by Louise Hay), was amenable to her request to rework some of her decks — replacing certain cards, no matter the expense. Moving forward, Colette will not be using any specific indigenous art and she removed a card depicting the Native American figure White Buffalo Calf Woman from her *Goddess Power Oracle*. 'Once I dove into the history of how the symbolic pipe was gifted to the Lakota tribe, I realised that I was not successful in being as respectful as I hoped. The Eagle King in *Wisdom of the Hidden Realms* had to go, too, and be replaced.'

Colette's *Wisdom of the Oracle* deck includes new, more diverse, card designs. 'I may be white but the world is not all white and this is part of the evolution of things,' she said. 'Yes, awkward; yes, difficult; but so what? If any progress is to be made, we need to get with the program and do our own work on this.'

Colette pointed to up-and-coming deck creators who are already wise to the importance of cultural awareness. 'Bottom line: there is nothing new in the New Age, including how all this plays out. I am committed to do my part to make the world a better place, to see unity in diversity and to be part of the positive changes that are happening and not expect everything to play out "nicely".

'If we really are "one" in spirit,' she continued, 'we need to dismantle whatever it is we're doing that doesn't support that. One imperfect, messy, awkward and joyful day at a time.'

A VISION AND A MARKETPLACE

I've attended my share of Mind Body Spirit (MBS) Festivals over the last decade, and at each one, I seem to set out invisible boundaries around what I will try. Partly because I'm more interested in a genuine experience than anything complicated or performative. But also, I'm not that adventurous; it can take years for me to try something. Spirit guide drawings are one of those things.

I'm not sure if it's the appropriation of shamanism, the creative yearning of the artist to draw someone with Native American looks, or both that has put me off. In a *This American Life* episode about drug use ('I Was So High'), many listeners who took hallucinogenic drugs said that they were greeted by a Native American. (See also *Wayne's World 2* for a plot line that sees Wayne, in his dream world, led by a Native American through the desert.)

These strange and borderline offensive representations underline my lack of interest in spirit guide drawings. But, for research purposes, I decide it's time.

I agree to meet my spirit guide with a kind-looking woman, Sharon, with an easel and a set of adult-sized crayons. I'm still recovering from a coffee cup reading an hour earlier (more research), where the man threw bundles of information at me that wasn't all wrong, but so general that it's hard to believe he was anywhere near as talented as the women in my lineage.

Sharon tells me she will find more than one guide and, like a contestant on a game show, I get to pick who I want to see. First, there's a woman, helping me connect with my spirituality and healing abilities. 'I can see you being very creative . . . and connecting with the animals. I could see you healing and connecting with people. And I could see you helping others but, at the same time, you were feeling good about who you were.'

Not a Native American woman at least.

'You also have a very strong Native American male as well, very much protected,' Sharon continues. This, she says, stands to reason because I'm a 'medicine woman', and my lineage goes as far back as Pleiadean times (think ancient aliens, because basically, I'm an ancient soul).

'I'll just travel a little while and then I'll stop,' Sharon says like she's taking me on a scenic tour of my soul's existence. 'I see you also enjoyed being a Celt . . . Interesting. I didn't expect to see that,' she says, with genuine surprise. 'You also have an Aboriginal, which is nice, too.' There are more, but these ones are the closest. 'So who would you like to see?'

I feel like I'm in a choose-your-own-adventure, but one that I know I was never going to really enjoy. I am polite, because Sharon is sweet and earnest. Even though I don't believe any of it, I do wonder if she genuinely does. I let her pick.

'I'll stand up and let them decide,' she laughs. 'You hand it to me, I hand it to them.' I wonder at this interesting, imaginative world she occupies.

We're going with the Celt. She offers to include any totem animals that appear. I agree, thinking if it's a dog, my canine-obsessed husband will never let me hear the end of it. She begins to scribble, tells me that my guide talks about my life as a teacher, and that I have many gifts that he wants to help bring out. He also instructs Sharon that I am an intuitive, creative, clever person, but that he has to wake me up at times.

Before I can get fully outraged, Sharon continues, a bit protective of spirit guide Judgey McJudgerson. 'There's a beautiful moment you could be embracing but you're always thinking, and, he says, "I'm helping you to be in the moment".'

On black cardboard, Sharon quickly renders an image of a man with sad eyes, a remarkable mane of hair and a white beard. He's olive-skinned and makes me think of Jesus. She adds a crown of leaves to his head. This, she tells me that he tells her, is because we used to sneak into the forest in a past life and camouflage ourselves in leaves. We would allow animals to gather around us, but we would sit perfectly still and just be in the moment.

Sharon draws an owl with impressively large wings outstretched. My totem animal.

'The owl tells me that you've got many gifts and abilities, which you already know, and it's just helping you to bring them to the fore. And he's helping you to be in the moment while you are bringing them to the fore.'

Sharon pauses to ask for a name for my spirit guide, the man with the sad eyes and mane of hair.

As an exercise, I decide to silently join in. Just as a name occurs to me, she speaks.

'I can almost get it,' she says. 'OK, I kept asking and it kept coming through. He said, "My name's Stone and they gave me the nickname in that lifetime because I was always strong and true." OK?' she says happily.

She senses that I'm less than enthusiastic about this odd name. 'Sometimes you get a name and you think, nah.'

'I was getting a name, but it was definitely not that.'

'Oh it might have been another version of it. What was your name?'

'Jeremiah, but I don't know why.' (True story.)

'Do you know why? Because that was his name in another lifetime,' she says quickly, before a pause. 'Jeremiah. I don't know that that's a Celtic name,' she says, genuinely at a loss, as though that's the hardest part to believe in all of this.

I walked away with a beautiful piece of art, even if it was rendered in crayons on a flimsy piece of cardboard. Sharon is a talented artist who has a belief and a gift she would like to share. While I don't believe a Celtic spirit guide named Stone follows me around, I do think she did. I also respect that spirit guides are a part of some sacred traditions, so I don't speak lightly about communicating with one. I am not sure what invisible beings, if any, shadow us but as someone who grew up being told we have shoulder angels (one to record our good deeds, the other our bad), it's not something I completely discount.

Later, I tell my husband Chris about Stone, and about needing to choose between the Celt and the Native American medicine man.

'What I want to know is,' Chris begins, 'why is it never a chain-smoking Nordic lesbian with bad teeth?'

'Give it time,' I say, thinking of just how gritty New Age can get because in an increasingly open and globalised world, it has to cater to everybody.

And perhaps that's what spirit drawings ultimately symbolise to me: the commodification of sacred tradition.

There is an undercurrent of greed in the modern New Age world. It can be flimsy and half-hearted. It's a place that doesn't manufacture miracles but sells the possibility of them, framed in a modern context even as the ancient or extremely old aspect to it is referenced for credibility. It is an industry after all, and despite its best efforts to exude love, light and purity, it's a profitable, money-making one. Economic analysis estimates that self-help alone is a multi-billion-dollar industry.

This is most notable with yoga — increasingly, this practice is being re-engineered and shopped to Westerners as an essential part of a wellbeing routine. The instructors are usually Westerners who rattle off *namastes* and terms for poses like pros. Often, they maintain Instagram accounts filled with yoga poses on a beach and trolley-loads of hashtagged blessings.

Stuart Weinberg, in his book *Crystals and the New Age*, summarises it well when he says that 'the New Age is both a vision and a marketplace'. It gathers together traditions both religious and spiritual in a 'nuanced and selective' way, crossing through science, and bringing in analytical and strategic tools for our wellbeing, and that of the planet and beyond.

And a marketplace? As I scroll through emails I subscribed to for the purposes of research I can only agree. Take, for example, the 21-day slew of emails offering galactic activations and quantum healing: imagination run wild, unearthly beings, guides and angels that are accessible with the right instructor for only $29.99. Consumers are not the only targets: even practitioners are encouraged to sign up for expensive courses with vague outlines and certifications.

I think about this when I see a major airline advertise Asia as a destination for adventure, spirituality and culture. As though spirituality is a place you visit, a temporary experience to be captured on social media, exit at the gift shop.

Similarly, I cringe at how retailers latch on to the Chinese New Year, advertising products in the colour red, or when I see Arabic patterns traditionally seen on men's headdresses worn as dresses. When I see people wearing a Palestinian *kuffiyeh* made in China, I think of all the Palestinian seamstresses and artisans whose work is stolen, whose income is affected because of mass production due to Western demand.

Another example is the abundant usage of Native American symbology and tradition. Dreamcatchers — a hoop with a weaving and feathers, and cultural significance — can include sacred objects, but they are so common now, you can find them in boxes with instructions on how to assemble your own. They are inextricably linked to New Age spaces, or perhaps more as an object that suggests spiritual endeavour. I have seen them on posters at variety stores, in airport shops as keyrings and in jewellery.

But the problem doesn't begin and end with cheap airfares and photogenic dreamcatchers. Writing for *Quartz* (qz.com), Roxanne Dunbar-Ortiz cites the example of celebrity self-help guru James Arthur Ray, feted by talk show hosts on US television at the height of his success in the noughties. His book *Harmonic Wealth: The Secret of Attracting the Life You Want* was a *New York Times* bestseller. To be individually mentored by him, writes Dunbar-Ortiz, could have set you back more than $90,000. A weeklong 'Spiritual Warrior' retreat in Sedona, Arizona, tapped in at almost $10,000.

Then tragedy struck when three people died in a sweat lodge ceremony Ray conducted, with eighteen people also hospitalised. Dunbar-Ortiz explains that protocols adhered to by Native spiritual leaders had been violated. Ceremonial acts require years of training, and sometimes an inherited right. The abuses included 'grossly incorrect construction of the lodge', misuse of herbs and other substances, and a lack of breaks to cool the lodge.

There was understandable outrage at the two-year sentence he received when he was convicted of negligent homicide for the deaths. Also, Dunbar-Ortiz writes, there was nothing to prevent him from running further sweat lodges.

A gathering of Lakota, Dakota and Nakota people led to a 'Declaration of War Against Exploiters of Lakota Spirituality', but that it has prevented non-Native Americans from corrupting traditional practices for monetary gain is not evident.

In the *Journal of Contemporary Religion*, Michael York suggests society's current spiritual pluralism is the result of a world turning away from traditional religion in favour of secularisation. 'From a New Age perspective, the world's various spiritual traditions are now public property and no longer the private preserve of the parochial groups or religious élites that they once were. Since in this open availability process, the sacred becomes commodified, the general argument allows that it can be bought and sold and thus consumed according to basic free-market principles.'

But even religions commodify their saints, offering experiences and blessed water at a cost. I would say most people aren't buying into New Age because they want to burn cash; they do it because they derive some kind of genuine benefit from their experiences. Not all commodified New Age practices are shallow or meaningless. Most things of value have a price tag; we just have trouble deciding when it's worth it.

Even in a secular world, people are looking for answers, or direction, possibly just a thread of hope and comfort that this isn't all there is. Beyond that, people are looking for relief. There is a reason why our bookshelves are bursting with such a multitude of New Age, self-help options: we have a lot of emotions to clear, experiences and people to forgive, things to unlearn and unfeel. But this is where I think consumers should tread softly in their pursuit of healing and relief; some things cannot be found in a book alone, if at all. And no matter what an author or healer or expert has gone through, their experiences do not necessarily mirror yours, nor the mechanics of how you put yourself back together.

I find myself reflecting frequently and carefully on the New Age's lack of newness. I agree with increasingly popular opinion that capitalism is evil, but I don't know anything with value for humans that hasn't been marketed. If it is useful, someone is going to sell it. If the demand for it exists and grows, more offerings will follow. So any marketplace gets polluted and will attract the snake oil salespeople.

But I know this space, know many of the people inhabiting it. They might be making a career out of what they offer, but so many are not careless or malicious in doing so. I do think that the New Age was born before people responded with complexity and sophistication to what it was offering to them. Nowadays, we are aware that the New Age is not all that new, and that sacred traditions have been liberally dunked into a commodified pool.

THE NEW AGE IS NO CULT

There's understandable scrutiny of the more extreme elements of the New Age — miracles for the ill or disillusioned; otherworldly experiences that cost a bomb; high-end self-help and spirituality that looks great with an Instagram filter but offers little in terms of authentic experience. And of course, like anything that demands allegiance or unwavering devotion, some aspects of the New Age veer dangerously close to cultish status — with leaders requiring allegiance to an idea or themselves (though this is not always the case), and people getting sold shit they don't need or an undercurrent of insecurity that will keep them tethered to the next big solution.

Alan Watts, English philosopher and expert in comparative belief systems, spoke humorously about the idea that humans require constant instruction through study of a particular modality. In his audiobook *Just So: An Odyssey into the Cosmic Web of Connection, Play, and True Pleasure,* he jokes that if he were to follow all of the varying pieces of advice on how to get himself 'into shape', his whole day would involve undertaking exercises 'in preparation for life'.

Then, he says, another school of thought will say he's getting confused: just do one thing. How to choose, though, asks Watts? 'Well, the person you're talking to will say their way is the best', but that could put you in the path of 'some religious fanatic'.

Watts grows a little more serious though: his hope is to set people free with knowledge, not wed them to continuous education.

It's rare to find offerings in the New Age marketplace that are one-off classes or sessions that set you up for life, or at least for a decent period of time before you have outgrown them. The biggest vulnerability lies in the swiftness with which a desire to feel better can mushroom into a way of life and an ever-expanding belief system. It seems to me that even the most elaborate or outlandish systems all begin with common sense. This is how it takes hold: recognisable, identifiable and universal points of pain, and solutions that range from reasonable to magical. Self-help will usher you through relationships (especially the one with yourself) and teach you how to, at times exhaustingly, think positive and change how you live. Spirituality will send you on a potentially feverish journey into the unknown to sate mystical longing and experience different physical and mental states in the process. The New Age may merge the two of them and offer adaptations of ideas in the forms of canons of knowledge and ancient wisdom.

In the New Age, therefore, we have guides and saviours of different kinds, and a unique language of love and light.

In any New Age sphere of MBS, there are people who are looking for genuine healing and solutions, and would perhaps be better served by medical or other professionals. I know practitioners who struggle with these conversations, but will have them: telling a client that they are not the right person to help them.

In her book *Zealot: A Book about Cults*, writer Jo Thornely seems to exhibit a similar sensibility: she recognises that people who are drawn into cults are looking for something to fill a gap; 'commonly they attract people whose current religion or lifestyle is lacking — it's too restrictive, it's not restrictive or pious enough, it doesn't seem to offer solutions for a chaotic and dangerous world, it doesn't let them have enough sex with aliens'.

I have heard and read things that cannot be unheard or unread: accounts of interdimensional travel that see demons trying to drag people out of their beds (not to be mistaken for sleep paralysis); sex with demons; magic that is darker than the night; drawn-out self-flagellation in allegiance to a belief system that seems to run on the smallness in us all. This is not the realm of religion or faith, it is the realm of humans, who scramble for a place in the world, for purpose and meaning. But I also see things of beauty; moments or extended periods of transcendence; synchronicity that lights up a person's creativity or mending process. These sorts of blissful experiences cross any kind of modality or practice. It's not the method but the journey you take.

Still, it's clear that we're also inundated with options and, quite possibly, going in circles to the point of confusion. Is the New Age a cult? No. There is no clear leader or devotion to a particular, single way of life or set of ideas. However, this is not to say it could never *contain* cults within it. I don't know of any that would fall under mainstream New Age, but some people would see certain practices as attracting a 'cult following' (such as a particular type of yoga or the latest health trend).

And you know the joke: what's the difference between a religion and a cult? The numbers. But that seems less true nowadays as religion and spirituality melt into each other.

While the New Age may have within it cliques and devoted cultish groups, so far they are not Jonestown-significant, and may simply have the markings of cult-like fervour. Religion, similarly, asks for devotion and allegiance to a way of life and a system of belief; major religions, with their big numbers, see a spectrum of behaviours, from the quietly observant to the offshoots that take on the qualities of a cult.

As Thornely writes in her book, much of the lure of a cult is a charismatic leader. The back story is important. You will find those in the hallways of all New Age modalities. Certainly, much of what you encounter is designed to lock you in, hence the advanced courses, upgrades and activations. But while I think it would be a stretch to say that a New Age guru is a cult leader, it can look cultish because of the followers' devotion. Like with celebrity fan-worship, the engagement becomes about the guru — attending every talk, buying every book and listening to every podcast — bypassing the original point, whether it be individuation, self-love, freedom, self-empowerment and so on. Mythology scholar Joseph Campbell said we are looking for the next parent in our lives when we latch on to a guru. The important thing to remember is that no one person or guide will always know what's best for you.

A virtuous conversion

In 2017, one of the big names in the industry, Doreen Virtue, sent shockwaves through the New Age world when her slow movement towards Christian-inspired messaging became her new business. She denounced her own previous canon of work — books, card decks and online courses that traversed the worlds of deities, angels, faeries and other invisible realm beings. From her property in Hawaii, where the vegan New Age superstar often rescues animals, she had previously been posting weekly oracle forecasts using her own decks. Upon her religious rebirth, rumours flooded the internet and oracle decks were junked in dismay. Had Virtue really said that her previously channelled work was 'demonically transmitted'? What of her online courses that gave students certificates in angel healing and the like? Was she crapping on her own extensive library of work, essentially saying it is all BS?

At first it seemed possible that she was simply making adjustments to her message, with a focus on Jesus (she even released a card deck for him). But then, in 2019, a post on her website popped up, 'An A–Z List of New Age Practices to Avoid, and Why'. She doesn't mince words in outlining the New Age practices people should avoid, throwing substantial shade at the fantastical promises of the New Age (ones she once happily played in) and their hidden dangers. These include energy healing, feng shui, following your bliss and even mindfulness.

I wonder if there are a lot of former followers of Virtue who are feeling sore and confused, especially given that a lot of New Age practices leave you feeling loved up, not like you've just raged with demons. And given that she was also the purveyor of training for oracle card readers around the world, some may be scratching their heads about that angel certificate they earned through a course.

All of this highlights the discord between traditional religion and the New Age, resulting in Virtue's entire rejection of the latter.

HOW WOO WOO ARE YOU?

At the Mind Body Spirit Festival in Sydney, I notice how convoluted the space has become. Once it was a quieter, more unusual and interesting group of people offering odd or just intriguing opportunities for healing, enlightenment and bliss. Now, between the juice stations, tea stands, Indigenous jewellery and psychic pit, you will also find mainstream religion. Catholics, Muslims and Scientology all have representation. One year I am sidelined by a representative from the Petersham Assembly of God Church, who also tells me that he is Jewish. (Only at MBS.)

Consider MBS a spectrum where modalities overlap. For example, self-help slides from giving practical advice on how to increase confidence to finding your soul purpose.

On one end of this spectrum are the dead-set rationalist/atheist/sceptic lot; on the other are ascended lightworkers who find invisible realms more interesting than the real one we inhabit.

Take a look at the different attitudes, beliefs and practices in each column of the table below, and work out where you sit.

Now, you may find yourself sitting in a particular spot

Woo-less	Woo-curious	Getting Woo-mer
Science is everything. I think horoscopes are silly, meditation is a waste of time, and New Agers are misguided. Some may call me a cynic, but I see myself as a realist.	I like to meditate and attend yoga classes. Books and podcasts about mindfulness appeal to me. You'll often find me perusing the self-help or spirituality sections of my local bookshop or streaming service. I've never had any kind of reading done, but might if it was offered to me.	I own at least one oracle or tarot card deck. I actively seek out New Age ideas, and am happy to pick-and-mix those that resonate with me. I may use crystals but don't feel the need to cleanse them under a full moon. I love essential oils but don't use them for spells.

on the spectrum, but that doesn't mean you're stuck there. Your position can change over time, and that's the beauty of the New Age and MBS. You may find yourself embracing things you once outright rejected, or vice versa; you may veer towards scepticism and pragmatism, then swerve towards more mystical pursuits and ideas, depending on where you are in life. And that's OK. It's all part of the journey.

It's a Woo-nderful Life	Woo-perman	Out of this Woo-ld
I maintain at least one regular spiritual practice. I go on retreats, and may even have a regular psychic. I am open to trying out new things, and want to be of service to the world. I use words like 'energy', 'vibration', 'resonate' and 'higher self'.	I have a guru or am otherwise devoted to a regular spiritual practice. I know what the Akashic Records are and believe in sacred contracts. I am on a first-name basis with my spirit guides. I own all the card decks, analyse my horoscope closely, and use crystals to heal.	My preferred sign-off is 'In love and light'. I have done a galactic activation and quantum tune-ups. I am also known by a name that starts with the title 'Priestess'. I am fluent in a light language.

CHAPTER TWO

Superstition, Sins & Spirits

I was raised in a cultural and religious world that is both ordinary and otherworldly, and this was both a challenge and a gift. On the one hand, my world was wide open in terms of metaphysical possibility; on the other, when you absorb supernatural belief through religion, it can be an 'all or nothing' deal — you get the comforting good stuff, but also a whole lot of pressure to never do wrong and to conform to groupthink.

There was tension between religion and culture as the daughter of Palestinian Muslim migrants living in the West. Now I can see quite clearly how my heritage provided structure but also restriction through religion. But I didn't think of it in these terms so explicitly when I was younger. These traditions and ways of thinking were just a part of my life, as normal as my obsession with movies and leg warmers. And while they required religious (at times dogmatic) belief, I think they provided the setting for who I was to become: a seeker interested in the esoteric.

One of the key lessons of my upbringing was that, in the everyday world, where many things are self-evident and provable, there is such a thing as magic, and superstition fuels it. While you drink coffee for enjoyment, it also contains clues to your day, month or even year ahead. Blue eye pendants and Hand of Fatima talismans or charms shield against *il ayn* (evil eye) and *hassad* (curse energy) and enchantments can yield positive transformation.

I remember being told strange things: that it was *haram* (forbidden) to whistle; that we shouldn't toss water out at night, or cut things (like hair or nails) after the sun went down. Later, I would discover the reasons 'why' — that throwing water out in the dark was risky because it could land on a jinn (which are generally invisible to humans), anger it and lead to harm. Ditto with the hair-cutting and whistling: you could unwittingly get the attention of jinn or cause harm to them.

In my family, we prayed daily (five times, though I often had to make up for my sunrise prayer later). We fasted during the month of Ramadan, according to the Islamic lunar calendar, which meant no food or drink (#notevenwater) from sunrise to sunset. We understood from a young age that religion involved a certain structure and restriction in areas that many of the people around us, primarily of European/Christian heritage, didn't experience.

Our beliefs were reflected in our daily lives in practical ways. We were taught invocations to use: to say *bismillah*

('In the name of God') before we eat and to finish our meals with *alhamdulillah* ('Thank God'). To never comment on someone's good fortune or looks without saying *masha'Allah* ('Praise be to God'), and to express contrition through the expression *astaghfir'Allah* ('God forgive us') when observing or committing a sin. The most commonly used one was *insha'Allah* (God willing), to be said for just about everything. Forget to say *insha'Allah* and the event you were so looking forward to might not happen. Neglect to praise God when complimenting someone and you could be inadvertently cursing them (or vice versa).

And so I added more to my vocabulary: *kafina shar* (a request to keep something bad away) and variations on 'God forbid' (touching wood occasionally for good measure). Meanwhile, a book of invocations instructed that you should only share good dreams with those you love. In the event of a bad dream, you were to dry spit over your left shoulder three times, saying with each repetition *'kafina shar min il helem'* — basically, a request to God to protect you from the dream. There are also a lot of sayings around the devil, designed to shield you from evil.

In most ways, being raised in religion was familiar, comforting and protective. Having an anchor in God was and continues to be a safe harbour. But it was a lot for a formative mind to take in, and there would be counterintuitive ramifications. Forgetting to say any of these invocations at the appropriate time would set off anxiety in me and I gradually developed a robust form of obsessive compulsive disorder, overanxious about reciting invocations, and ensuring I never said something that would offend God.

This is, interestingly, a condition I see in the New Age with the 'power of thought' police who guilt you for having the occasional negative ideas.

As I grew older, the rules would mushroom. Innocuous things became more complex: interactions between the sexes, purification rituals and what makes you unclean, and even how you enter the bathroom — your left foot goes in first, but when putting on your shoes, it's right before left.

I became more anxious over the years, worried all the time, hyper aware of my belief system, and too young to understand that the thing religion should first and foremost give us is a sense of peace because we have faith. I don't pin my OCD on religion; I think it simply gave it form. I would have those issues no matter what, because anxiety is a condition and it will find suitable outlets.

On reflection though, even as I suffered anxiety about doing things the right way, I did also find peace in my faith. It offered relief through prayer. My mother reciting Quran for me would never fail to reassure and calm me because I always felt safe in my mother's presence. Her Arabness and her devotion to religion never felt overwhelming; they were a comfort.

No matter how I evolve or shift along the spectrum of woo woo, and no matter how much I value my solitude, I could never go through life believing there is nothing greater than me, that we are without divine forces. I have something to hold onto, even if I don't always understand how or why this trust works.

The Arab and the Islamic parts of my existence have always complemented each other, though in some ways they can seem to contradict, too. Pure faith in God and His boundless mercy coinciding with a prickliness about the smallness of humans, with their envy and thirst for power, and the significance of invisible forces — and how they can harm you.

In other ways, I had a very 'normal' childhood by Western measurements — Mum gifted me my first Barbie doll at an appropriate tween age. I had a wild imagination that allowed me to turn an ordinary grocery box into a doll's dream house. I watched American films and TV shows, went to public school, then crushed on boy bands and actors as I leaned into my adolescence.

But I also had this filter. One that saw me edge my way along some thin cultural lines. I was surrounded by people who had a variety of, at times conflicting, approaches to life. My Greek friends were perhaps the ones I felt closest to in cultural terms. Like me, they ate 'different' food, they weren't allowed to go to sleepovers, and religion and super-stition played a role in their lives.

We all grow up with various religious, cultural and familial traditions and symbols — some more so than others. Here are a few of the symbols and beliefs that loomed large in my formative years, and that are now popular in the New Age and beyond.

THE EVIL EYE (AND OTHER BAD THINGS)

New Age circles focus on thrilling ideas like 'low vibrational energy' and 'energy vampires'. They invest in elemental mythologies, tapping into nature spirits and other invisible creatures like faeries, unicorns and dragons. I have read books dedicated to how to honour elementals — beings like sylphs and gnomes — and how to protect yourself from psychic attack, or from invisible travellers from other realms when undertaking ritual. It's not light reading, and people take it very seriously. But for someone born into a world of mystical possibility, it's also just not that unusual to me. Take, for instance, the evil eye, a form of 'psychic attack' or negative vibes sent your way, and the rituals that help to ward it off or rid you of it.

In my household, the evil eye became more of a focus, and interest, as I moved through my twenties. It's not something my mother talked specifically about in my childhood, but it was a part of the tapestry of my life even outside my home. I would notice things. That Arabs safety-pinned a little blue eye to a baby's jumpsuit. That we weren't supposed to share too much about our lives to other people in case they became envious. That my mother holding me and reciting Quran could deliver instant relief and an impenetrable sense of safety, the fog of fear lifted. And of course, we were taught those invocations and supplications.

I was once at a social gathering, in a lovely apartment where guests earnestly praised the host's impressive bookshelves crammed with titles old and new, and a large, beautiful vase crashed to the ground. One guest laughingly appraised the situation: '*Kassar il shar*'.

This saying, *kassar il shar*, means 'it broke the evil eye'. It's a bit lumbering in English but we say it when something breaks, shattering the heavy energy that comes with someone's bad intentions against you, dispelling the heaviness of their envy or ill will. The saying is also used in reference to rituals that dispel the evil eye; things like burning sage, reciting invocations to God, or undertaking village remedies. Nothing too outlandish. No animals are harmed in the making of your common evil eye remedy. But really, at the most basic level, you've got to be a believer.

Another term you hear flung about is *hassad*, which is envy running at a deeper level, worse than your everyday jealousy. I have always thought of *hassad* as a deliberate curse. While *ayn* can come from anyone, including those who love you (i.e. they don't intend harm, but they are jealous or complimentary towards you without praising God), *hassad* is more intentional. It's a hardcore bad vibe that comes from someone who dislikes you, or who wants what you have (or for you not to have it).

Judging by the number of blue eye pendants and amulets on sale around the world, the evil eye is a popularly held belief. It is certainly a common element of many religions and mythologies, and I have discovered striking similarities between what Muslims and others say to ward off evil and protect themselves from the darkness of others' hearts. Arabs, Greeks, Italians, Asians, South Americans and many more have their ideas about luck and curses, and all have some variation of the evil eye superstition. In Turkish restaurants, Arabic grocery stores and the homes of most ethnic minority families you'll find blue evil eye talismans or Hand of Fatima and Khamsa amulets. Like crystals, they're meant to protect you — they absorb bad energy, and one day will most likely break when they have done their work on your behalf.

There is more than one way to rid yourself of the evil eye. The Greeks use oil. Native Americans use sage. In Mexico, a friend told me, the eye is often manifested as 'bad air'. 'So people often won't touch a baby immediately after entering the house if they were out in public. First they wash their hands and wait a while for the bad air to dissipate,' she told me. And, like Arabs, they are extra protective of babies. Muslims can say prayers to ward off negative vibes from anyone, but they are particularly protective of young ones.

The Islamic faith even has protective prescriptions (recitation of Quranic verses or brief invocations, for example) because it accepts magic and evil eye as real, however, it is *haram* (forbidden) to partake in it. I have distinct memories of a little brass cup that belonged to my mother, inscribed with Quranic verses, tucked between the teacups and sage in the kitchen cupboard. We would drink water from it when feeling afraid or in need. But Mum mainly did (and continues to do) the prayers, which we call *ruqqiyah*. Some people read three specific verses of the Quran three times each for a person, placing their hand on the afflicted person's head (though you can also read for yourself).

Writing for Dubai-based newspaper *The National*, Art Correspondent Melissa Gronlund considered the significance of the evil eye, so iconic that it's moved beyond being a centrepiece for jewellery or decoration — it's now a bona fide emoji.

'The idea of the evil eye is impressively ancient,' Gronlund reports, noting that its image has been found in Sumerian cave drawings, Syrian amulets from 3000 BC, and even in the ancient Roman poetry of Virgil. And while amulets are a market stall staple today, their origin is reported to be from the Ottoman Empire.

If carrying around an amulet isn't your thing, there are various village remedies, though some may admittedly be questionable from an OH&S point of view. I knew a Lebanese woman whose family melted candle wax into a bowl of water and then read the shapes to divine what was behind a bout of bad luck or negative energy.

In my twenties, there was a time when I was feeling particularly down. Despite the many blessings of safety, home and work, life felt stagnant. Friends I'd grown up with were travelling and finding partners, moving forward and I was feeling lost, lonely and depressed. I would cry often, and my mother felt I needed supercharged protection. She upped the Quranic recitations to seven each in one sitting, adding a long invocation of protection at the end, running her hands from head to toe in front of my body. This was to offer comfort (tick), but I think Mum wondered at my odd sadness. On the surface of things, life was not greatly exciting, sure, but it didn't warrant such dark feelings. The prolonged nature of my downward spiral led us to attempt a village remedy in case some of my bad juju was coming from somebody harbouring negative feelings about me. You never know what can set off jealousy in another person.

We didn't use candle wax; this ritual required metal and fire. More specifically, melting a small ball of lead in a metal bowl over the head of the afflicted.

I trotted off to the nearest Kmart and headed straight to the fishing department. Doubt about the ritual tugged at me, but I was desperate, so my only challenge was determining what size tackle would be suitable. Growing excited about the magical work we were about to do, I suggested to Mum that we innovate, feeling inspired by the candle wax ritual. 'Let's put the molten lead into water and see what shapes it forms!'

Mum only knew the ritual and was reluctant to read the shapes, but she agreed. She proceeded to melt the lead into a bowl over my head, reciting Quran and invocations as she did so. I can't remember if I cried. Usually, if Mum did *ruqqiyah*, I would bawl my eyes out — a true sign that I had been evil-eyed and the cleansing was doing its work. But I think I was more nervous than teary. One wrong move and I'd be wearing a new headpiece.

When the lead was melted down, Mum poured it into a bowl of water. The tackle ball was small, so we weren't about to get a hero's journey told in several acts. Instead, we deciphered a small, but very distinct, rat. There was a snout, the plump body, and the little tail. A name for the person the rat was meant to symbolise would have been grand, but I was going to take what I could get.

Mum and I threw up some possibilities. A rat is certainly not an auspicious animal to see in your evil eye metal. Rats are unattractive, dirty and sneaky. Although intelligent, and symbolic of wealth and success in Chinese culture, it was not an animal I wanted to see show up when dispelling the evil eye. I mean, whose animal guide is ever a rat?

While you can ward against the evil eye and other curses, if you are subjected to either, the desire would be to dispel it. But sometimes it's neither *ayn* or *hassad*. It's possession, stories of which will keep even the stoniest adult awake at night. Relatives have regaled me with tales of spirits taking the form of humans populating our spaces. One woman I know was paralysed in her bed for extended periods of time by the presence of men in black in the room. Later, I wondered if this was sleep paralysis, where a person is aware but can't move or communicate, and may experience similar halluci- nations. Regardless, it would have been terrifying.

Then there are the stories of people being possessed and the exorcisms undertaken by clerics or other religious folk. A very devout Muslim friend during my university days talked about witnessing them. She was matter of fact — possession is real, but you really don't want to see one. I didn't need any convincing on that.

Of course, the best way to avoid or disempower the evil eye or other curses is to reject the possibility of their existence altogether. Simply don't acknowledge them as a reality. Tune into the positive and veer away from the formation of something negative and burdensome. But if, like me, you are attuned to superstition, feel like you need to have a shower after you've spent time with someone who makes you feel off, or are even partial to a ghost story or two, on some level you accept that evil eye can be a 'thing', and it may encroach on your life if you let it.

JINN (AND THE UNSEEN)

It's not simply the evil or malevolent glare of other humans that people shield against or fear. Many cultures hold beliefs around unseen forces and beings. Throughout my travels in Europe and even the Middle East, I have marvelled at the pantheons of gods and goddesses on display, all of whom tell us stories about what it means to be human. Unlike monotheistic deities, they seem less about fear and more about reverence.

Arab tradition and history is steeped in mythology that is accepted as fact: pre- and post-Islamic Arabia are upheld by a belief system that carries stories of supernatural forces influencing the fates of people. These supernatural creatures — commonly known as genies, spirits or demons — are called jinn.

Jinn exist in the imaginal realm. They are shape-shifters, can be tricksters, and are intelligent beings. They are rational, responsible and have free will. They can be sedentary or nomadic. They have characteristics similar to those of faeries and other magical creatures in various traditions. In a way, they seem to exist as an allegory for humans and their behaviours. Like humans, their allegiance to God is also put to the test, and Islam speaks of jinn of different nations, formed of tribes. There can be Muslim jinn or Jewish jinn, for example, so they are capable of accepting the word of God.

They also interrelate with, and infiltrate the human world. They are powerful, but humans are superior. They are eternal travellers between realms (seen and unseen), and are proof that our physical reality is not the sole one. They disappear into darkness, receding into invisible worlds, only to unexpectedly appear again.

The jinn, very importantly, are capable of good or evil. They are made of fire and air; the humans are earth and water. They can see us but generally, we can't see them, though if they shapeshift into the form of an animal, human or something else tangible, we see them in that form.

In *Islam, Arabs, and the Intelligent World of the Jinn*, Amira El-Zein offers an academic but concise history of the evolution of the ideas around jinn. Simply put, jinn existed in the community consciousness long before Islam warned its followers against dealing with them. Islam did not distinguish but rather reinforced the existence of jinn, embracing the idea of invisible worlds and the existence of spirits that are otherworldly but behave and are judged by God similarly to humans.

Islam is infused with mystical concepts and energies. It emphasises, for example, that Allah is 'Lord of the Worlds' — meaning that Allah created multiple worlds, some of which can be visited in a transcendent state. For example, there is a 'white' universe in Islam that El-Zein says embodies 'transcendence and purity', with days 30 times longer than those on Earth, and where its inhabitants are not aware of disobedience towards God.

In some ways, this clarifies some confusion about superstition and religion: the beliefs around supernatural forces in Arab world mythology, with its particular focus on jinn and religious ideology, both reinforce and contradict ideas around magic, fate and supernatural forces.

While Islam acknowledges that magic is real and can cause genuine harm, it forbids sorcery. The only way Islam allows for magical influences is through Islam itself. There is much debate about what is permissible and what isn't, but it's unlikely that someone would argue that reciting verses of the Quran to counter a spell or black magic against someone would be wrong.

Regardless, many Muslims comfortably flit between religion and magic when they undertake rituals to undo evil eye and the like — their belief in magic is tied to their religious beliefs so the lines about what is permissible get blurred. Arabs love their village remedies (such as the Quranic recitations, or melting a ball of lead while doing this) but these could arguably fall under sorcery. In essence, anything that calls on the power of beings other than Allah would be considered not only *haram* (forbidden), but also possibly *shirk* (partnering God with others, the greatest sin in Islam). Yet I know many Muslims who comfortably undertake such rituals.

Arabic folklore is interesting but not unique in the belief system it upholds. The Celts have the fae and elementals, powerful beings connected to the energies of nature and the elements. Graeco-Roman magic favoured mythology that embraced gods and goddesses, and even witches. Rituals, spells and amulets were important in ancient Egypt. And in the New Age, all of these have a place at the table.

The divine feminine

As in many parts of the world, a spiritual life in ancient Arabia contained a balance of feminine and masculine devotion. The pre-Islamic era saw many Arab priestesses who were considered very powerful. Seers were believed to have their own jinn, with women seers being more easily taken by these spirits, communicating through their bodies and speaking through their lips.

With the advent of Abrahamic faiths in the East, the divine feminine was discarded and a masculine, patriarchal mindset took hold to guide society. Islam sought finally to shed the Arab world of its pagan roots and no longer was there a divine feminine influence.

Despite the social inequalities between men and women at the advent of Islam, Arabs revered and worshipped goddesses as well as gods. The goddesses included al-Lat, al-'Uzza and Manat. They are mentioned in the Quran, so their names are still known, but core to Islam is the acceptance that God is one and that the Prophet Muhammed was His final messenger. The *shahadah* (declaration of faith) is literally: 'There is no God but God, and Muhammed is His final messenger'.

While Islam introduced rights for women that they had previously been denied (such as being able to own property and certain changes to marriage and inheritance), there is no denying that the Islamic world centres men. Even when speaking about the rights of women, it is men deciding what these are. Of course, I know many Muslim women who find their freedom in practice. This is important: we have the right to choose how we go through this world. Or, we should, so long as it does not cause actual (rather than perceived) harm.

As an adult, I find this history intensely fascinating and instructive, navigating a deeply patriarchal world. It raises questions about how belief shapes society, or vice versa. This is particularly evident in today's New Age: a pick-and-mixing of belief that reflects who we are and what we want. And what we *want* is to feel connected to unseen forces. It's no surprise that goddesses are seeing a return among women, steering us towards a more balanced idea of divinity and humanity's relationship to it. Indeed, a return of the 'divine feminine' seems to be having a wave effect around the world, with an explosion of goddess circles, oracle decks, rituals and pagan pathways. This is reflected in the secular world too, with movements like #metoo and #timesup.

RITUAL AND SUPERSTITION

But what is superstition anyway? Does it have legs? From drawing luck through a talisman, to warding against the effects of an energy vampire, we often feel the need to protect ourselves. We are nimble and cautious, at the mercy of an uncaring, unjust universe, whose natural laws we don't fully comprehend.

In the book *The Three Questions*, Toltec wisdom writers Don Miguel Ruiz and Barbara Emrys attempt to loosen superstition's hold on humans. Ideas can determine how we think and behave, they assert, saying superstitions can be more subtle than religious and cultural tales. 'Superstitions corrupt human imagination,' they warn, interestingly in the chapter titled 'Peace and sanity'.

I'm not attempting to encase all religion, spirituality and magic in superstition. But it's important to appreciate the undercurrent that superstition represents — fear, power-lessness and a desire to control our days and our destinies. With that comes ritual. I don't like the hold superstition can have on us, but there is something to the comfort a good ritual provides.

And it's fair to say that we are big on ritual in the Arab world. There is something highly appealing about ritualistic practice. It takes you out of yourself; it doesn't necessarily lead to a trance state, but with solid intention and clarity of purpose, performing a ritual can transform something within you.

'Both magic and religion depend on ritual to maintain cosmic order,' writes author Susan Greenwood in her book *The Encyclopedia of Magic & Witchcraft*. Belief and ritual work together, creating a cosmic bubble. This bubble can also be punctured if one — the belief or the ritual — is abandoned.

When I was younger, I don't think I fully appreciated or embraced this world of magical possibility, I just accepted it as part of life. I didn't completely comprehend it, either, a situation I have spent much of my adulthood attempting to rectify.

Ritual remains an important part of my life. We all have rituals in our lives, often so small and well-practised that we don't think of them in this way — blowing out candles on a birthday cake, or something you *always* say or do before a particular event. I have a few pre-festival rituals as a writer in the public eye. I'm reminded of my mother's comforting recitations from the Quran. You can't experience what I did and not feel the power in it. Was it simply my mother's love that transformed me? Who cares? In those moments when she would place a hand on my head and recite prayers on my behalf, something magical happened.

Given society's longstanding obsession with both super-stition and ritual, it's no wonder that they permeate the

New Age world. They are often reflective of traditional religious or other sacred practices. Perhaps esteemed scholar Joseph Campbell put it best when he explained ritual as 'the enactment of a myth'. Myths are all about truth, about showing us who we are or who we can be. Rituals deliver the same wisdom. Something is let go or unleashed. Depending on your beliefs or ideas, you are possibly communing with unseen forces. It does not have to be transcendent, but you are changing your emotional state.

The power isn't in knowing how it works. Ritual is meant to be transformative. It usually involves having an intention — a desire to understand something, or change it. You change your state to alter your view and comprehension. Perhaps it settles you so that you can more clearly see what next steps to take in a situation. It can simply be a balm to a troubled soul. It can break mental chains and unlock doors. I know this has been true for me, and I know this is the case for many others.

FLYING OUT OF THE CAGE

From my perspective, across all religions, beliefs and cultures, however you do life is how you do religion and belief. I spent my twenties hiding from the world, diving into religion, trying very hard to be more passionate about it than I actually felt, and linking it heavily to my identity. I call it my 'fundy days' (i.e. fundamentalist), that period many people have of turning to inherited religious practice and belief. I was fairly devout — I wore a headscarf, I didn't date boys, and I played everything pretty safe. Did I mention that I was still living at home and thought my future path revolved around getting the marriage thing right? Having kids? Playing it safe? It was a self-constructed bubble in some ways. My parents wanted the things most parents desire for their kids — an education (law), a good partner (marriage), and security (a safe life). I think my lack of interest in the many suitors who came to visit confounded my father, but I didn't feel pressured.

This was, in so many ways, my bubble, but it was based on what I had understood my place in the world to be growing up Arab and Muslim. My parents are less religious than many of the people I spent time with in my twenties. They are practising Muslims, but I see the influence of culture on how they behave and think, rendering them more conservative at times than 'religious'. I was more devout than they were at one point, referring to scripture and getting strict on my diet and behaviours in ways my family never has. When I recently assessed my parents this way directly to my mother, she rejected the 'conservative' label before a cheeky grin formed. 'We pick and choose,' she said with a laugh, and the skies opened above me.

My parents weren't always this way. But, like a cliff face worn down by waves crashing against it, having adult children who constantly test your boundaries will change the shape of things.

When I was younger, I was less inclined to ask questions that could lift me outside my bubble. I was unwilling to test the boundaries and find out how much of what I believed to be true about my potential and what life held for me was actually real. I was delaying the inevitable: the bubble eventually has to pop. A fundy approach will eventually dissipate; it's too intense and exhausting, unless you are a person of extremes in general. It's the puffed-up, confected moments of adherence that really don't last. Your character stays with you. But the things I did because I felt I had to, which didn't necessarily sit right, would eventually stop being of importance to me.

The first time I really stepped outside of the traditional practices was in my early thirties, a decade I slid into filled with disappointment and angst about a lack of achievement, fulfilment and purpose. I was still living at home with my folks, arguing about curfew. Mum, who likes to watch her stories into the night, would patiently listen as I unburdened myself beside her on the couch. One night, she pulled out a copy of *You Can Heal Your Life* by Louise Hay. It was in this moment I realised how — despite her devotion to religion — my mother has an open, exploratory mind. She is interested in the unseen — in all its forms — not just a believer in it.

And so, to my great surprise, it was my mother who set me on a path to self-help, something I had always scoffed at, but which unlocked a whole other world for me. By then, I had taken off the headscarf, but in many ways, I still lived like I was wearing it. That is to say, I was still a bit uptight, not easily trusting in the flow of life. Looking back now, I can see that I was a flightless bird, locked in a grand cage I had built for myself. It was time to step outside and alter the view.

CHAPTER THREE

Help Yourself

The more mystically inclined speak of a phenomenon called Saturn's Return. It happens first when you're 29 — your world is turned upside down, you (metaphorically) chuck out the old to let in the new, and you kind of try to figure out your mission statement for life. It happens again in your older years, but even if you don't subscribe to such mystical ponderings, the idea is reflected in the seven-year-itch-type deal. Seven years calls for a rebirth of sorts, and we constantly usher in change.

And so, when my mother introduced me to Hay's *You Can Heal Your Life,* I rolled my eyes but didn't completely ignore the sign. That's what it felt like. A gentle nudging to think differently, to open my mind to other ways of being in the world. I had reached my pain threshold and needed to bust out of the cocoon.

Sure, I grew up with that ether of belief in the supernatural, where spirits in the form of jinn were not myth. Where your whole life was a test that would land you in heaven or hell. I could handle that. But spouting affirmations? Getting in touch with my feelings? Looking in the metaphorical mirror to assess myself without fear of punishment? What kind of madness was this?

Hay's was the kind of book I was embarrassed to admit I was reading; I hid the cover on public transport. It seemed more suited to Americans who wear their hearts on their sleeves, who share deeply personal experiences with Dr Phil or Oprah.

Regardless, I decided to give Hay a chance. Her premise is that how we think and deal with the events and people in our lives impacts how we feel. But, and this is very important, she also argues that illness — aka 'dis-ease' — stems from something being out of balance in our lives. Hay suggests that the bad things that happen to us may be our own creations. And I should say, 'bad things' are on a sliding scale. For me, my problems paled in comparison to many others, but you know, we still have things to do, problems to sort through, despair to manage at varying levels. I try not to discount anything I or another goes through by comparing it. Some things are not comparable, but they can all be real with true effects on our wellbeing.

My bad stuff was pretty common and ordinary: trying to find love or being heartbroken; struggling with weight; managing unhealthy relationships; suffering low self-esteem and so on.

Given this stuff happens to all of us in varying ways,

was there really something to the idea that whatever shit happens in life is at our own hands? I'm not sure I could stomach that. It's a horrible accusation to lob at someone who is suffering or has experienced trauma. Also, could such thinking provoke a person to second-guess every thought and action? It did, however, make sense as a base thought in self-help: how can you convince people that they have power, that it's real and that they control their narrative if you also tell them they're a victim of life and chance?

While the affirmations are cheesy, they're not entirely lacking in wisdom. Hay tells you to consider your thoughts and speech as food for your brain, and you start to see that it makes sense to treat both with some compassion and positivity: *I am a positive and happy person!* Now say it and repeat it until you believe it.

It was an uneasy connection for me, because it seemed a bit twee, and I was sceptical that repeating an idea mentally or aloud would alter my reality. But one thing led to another and I got on board. Affirmations never stopped sounding cheesy to me, but I started listening to them. In my search for affirmative guidance, I stumbled upon a meditation expert online named Stin Hansen whose voice was soothing and reassuring to an unsettled mind.

A couple of years after my mother first introduced me to Hay, I saw how much I was changing over time. I was getting healthier in my mind and body; I was working in a job I enjoyed and was good at, surrounded by supportive co-workers. After listening to the forgiveness affirmations a few times, I randomly ran into a person I had a regretful dispute with several years ago. We easily reconnected and forgave the rift.

Reading Hay marked an important period for me, one of exploration that forced me to displace my cynicism about self-help and the New Age more generally. It's not simply that words like 'frequency', 'vibration' and 'energies' crept into my vocabulary. I needed something to change. I needed to learn to 'love myself' (though I would eventually realise that I didn't even 'like' myself). And I needed to want more for myself than I was taught to want. I had to move out of home; curfew at 30 wasn't cutting it.

I didn't become a voracious reader of these self-improvement and spiritual books; I found myself gravitating towards practical, ritualistic work. I started to play with oracle cards, and I attended weekly meditations with energy intuitive Denise Jarvie. I listened to affirmations, and I worked with healers who introduced me to interesting ways of letting go of baggage and paving a new way forward.

But all the while, a little voice hummed doubts in my ear. I was never going to be full woo woo and flout it; I was too self-conscious. I didn't mind sharing my ideas with certain people, and often people with similar views would share their experiences with me. A lot of the time, I was slamming down any sense of certainty with questions and assessment. I was yet to piece together how the mystical stems of my own religious upbringing would link to my New Age experiences. I did not yet understand how heavily derivative the New Age is, nor did I appreciate that it was becoming a massive industry based on existing cultural and religious traditions.

If something in my life improved, I wondered: was that always going to happen and I just found an easier way to bide my time with the rituals? Am I just feeling better because all of this 'work' forces me to place my focus elsewhere? That, it turns out, does help in distracting you from what makes you feel like shit.

And this is where I started to see how synchronicity and intuition rise when you're in a sort of 'flow'. You start to find solutions, and often in a moment of good timing. I was gradually becoming more receptive to trying out things that didn't always find mainstream acceptance. For example, a friend mentioned in conversation how hypnotherapy was helping her. I was sceptical about it, but felt a gentle tug to explore its possibilities. I decided to give it a try. I went in having no idea how it would work or if it would be effective. But in my first session I told my therapist that I wanted to move out of home.

Three months later, I did. And there was no force. Just a conversation where I laid down a complaint, then a suggestion, to my father. I knew that Arab-Muslim women didn't leave home before marriage, but a loophole dawned on me: I'd move in with my brother Hossam, who was already living alone. (I hadn't asked him yet, but I didn't slow down long enough to question it.)

Hypnotherapy simply involves talking out your feelings. My therapist wrote everything down, then she led me into a session where she relayed certain affirmative statements to me as though the thoughts were my own. This, of course, is in a near-trance state, so you're more susceptible to what is being said. But as my therapist explained, you can't be hypnotised to be or do something outside of your nature.

Did she create that next step with me? Or did it just ease my way towards an inevitable and challenging shift? I'm inclined nowadays to favour the latter. Around the same time, a lovely tea leaf reader I know, Lindel Barker-Revell, had read for me and told me I would be moving forward in life, 'coming and going' as I pleased. I didn't quite believe it, but then . . . life six months later looked remarkably different.

That said, I still had a lot of work to do on myself. For *ELLE*, I wrote about moving out of home and how it took a while before I started to act like I had this independence I'd won. I had moved out as a single Arab-Muslim woman, but I acted like someone who still lived with a curfew and ever-watchful, anxious parents. It was time to grow up, figure out who the hell I was, or perhaps rather, who I could be.

I truly believe that my openness to more affirmative thinking exposed me to new possibilities in my life. And I mean 'exposed' — I don't know that it 'created' or 'manifested' anything that wasn't already there. I didn't let it take over, or control me.

My intuition became more important to me, as well as understanding and reshaping my goals and desires. I went from being someone who thought her entire world should relate to being a wife and mother, to someone who craved solitude and freedom. I had emotional work to do, and I needed to learn to trust myself and my instincts more.

On reflection, I can see how I resisted the pull towards

the esoteric, but eventually it becomes too challenging to ignore natural inclinations. I am a restless soul, a spiritual wanderer whose life is very much centred on a creative, hopefully healing, path. It became too difficult to ignore that I was drawn to the mysteries of life, and experiences that are joyful and transformative. It was clear every time I entered a woo woo bookstore in Sydney and played with the oracle decks, in the way guided meditations became a weekly appointment. My life was slowly but surely finding new ways of spiritual exploration, connection and expression.

We've established that there is crossover between spirituality and self-help in the New Age, understandable given that this New Age is not new at all. But while the notion of self-help can make people cringe (including myself, who can see that sometimes it's very useful), I think it's still separate enough that it can accommodate people low on (or absent from) the woo woo spectrum.

Self-help is best known for its focus on positive thinking. It can help you find greater purpose, or change the way you think about life and opportunity. It can offer practical advice and solutions, and point out where we fall down, sometimes with quirky and therefore memorable names and terminology. It considers relationships, including the one you have with yourself. It tries to offer ways to help people heal from trauma or overcome their perceived limitations, to be more compassionate and forgiving. If you want to find your life purpose, to build your career or your confidence, if you feel like poor self-esteem is holding you back, self-help's shelves have plenty of options.

Take, for example, Gay Hendricks, who speaks of 'conscious growth'. In his book *The Big Leap*, he writes about the self-imposed 'Upper Limit Problem' that humans have when it comes to living a fulfilling life. He is essentially talking about self-sabotage. He also refers to a 'zone of genius'. His writing is infused with trust in a higher being, but it fits comfortably in self-help alongside less woo woo options, like Tony Robbins, a favourite with entrepreneurs and the wealthy. Robbins is all about a more masculine devotion to transformation and greatness. He instructs people to unleash, awaken and transform.

Self-help and transformational writers are usually looking for catchy ways to tell you how to live and feel better. If the title of the book or seminar isn't sappy and well-meaning or, in the other extreme, brutal, it is radical. Because forgiveness, acceptance and growth must never be ordinary.

They also manage quite well to identify frustrating human behaviours that will see you nod in agreement, primarily through acknowledging their own experiences. In *The Big Leap*, Hendricks, for example, neatly summarises human projection, which is so often at the heart of our problems: past experience has shown him that you will start to see in other people the feelings you have hidden inside of you that you don't know how to manage. So you try to manage it in others. Who isn't guilty of some good old projection once in a while? One of the most important results of my adventures in seeking is that I have learned ways to look inward, gazing into that metaphorical mirror so that I can have an honest relationship with myself and not spend time trying to fix or bother other people.

One of the most influential writers for me has been Don Miguel Ruiz, whose works *The Mastery of Love* and *The Four Agreements* (and a cheeky follow-up, *The Fifth Agreement*) helped me to unpack a lot of my ordinary and common beliefs that were harming my growth. His views are based on Toltec wisdom, and the first time I encountered his work with *The Mastery of Love*, certain things clicked into place for me about what it really means to 'love yourself'. His keen focus on the importance of being on good terms with yourself clarified for me why romantic relationships can be problematic or downright disastrous. Too often — and we have popular stories to thank in part — we see relationships as a fix, an ending to pain or confusion. Reading Ruiz solidified for me how important it is to exist in the world as yourself, knowing who you are as best as possible so that you don't compartmentalise yourself to accommodate others. That is, just be your friggin' self and find someone who is similarly just themselves and doesn't need you to change to make them feel better. Simple, right? Apparently not.

I guess the first step is acknowledging you have something to overcome, whether it's low self-worth, isolation, or shame and guilt.

We all operate on subtext. Learn to spot yourself. The way you self-sabotage can be quite remarkable.

Does anything stand the f*ck out?

Self-help is often maligned for being overly heartfelt and sincere. You may have noticed a shift of late in how it is being sold to people. An abundance of titles on bookstore shelves, all trying to help you overcome your bullshit to secure a wonderful life, but they are from the cooler, newer kids on the block. None of this love and light business; it's all about curing victimhood with no-nonsense, profanity-laden instruction. The most famous authors in the space are Mark Manson (*The Subtle Art of Not Giving a F*ck*) and Sarah Knight (*The Life-Changing Magic of Not Giving a F*ck*).

A tour of a major bookstore will deliver an array of other colourful titles that are centred on better living with a cool edge:

*Harden the F*ck Up* by Felix Economakis;
*F*ck Feelings* by Dr Michael Bennett and Sarah Bennett;
*F*ck It: Be at Peace With Life, Just As It Is* by John C.
    Parkin;
*How to Stop Feeling Like Sh*t* by Andrea Owen;
*Get Rich, Lucky B*tch* by Denise Duffield-Thomas;
And my favourite: *Unf*ck Yourself* by Gary John Bishop.

WHERE IT ALL BEGAN

Self-help has its roots more firmly in friendly life advice, often with Christian undertones. Think Norman Peale, Joseph Murphy, Dale Carnegie and later, Stephen Covey. Self-help, after all, came out of the US, even if its origins are arguably much older. Many will suggest that Louise Hay's main achievement in *You Can Heal Your Life* was introducing the world to positive thinking, but I think that she was more instrumental in establishing self-help as an industry, taking the baton from Dale Carnegie's *How to Win Friends and Influence People*. Hay may also be held responsible for the industry's sappiness; her affirmations are from another era, before sarcasm became the new self-help: 'It is safe for me to create all the love I want.'

In his book *50 Self-Help Classics*, Tom Butler-Bowdon covers 50 of the most formative self-help titles that he deems classics. Interestingly, his selections affirm the blurred lines between spirituality and self-help, and how these overlap in the New Age. He includes the Bible and the Bhagavad-Gita (under 'making a difference', alongside Brené Brown's *Daring Greatly*). Also featured are the big names of modern self-help and spiritual worlds: Tony Robbins' *Awaken the Giant Within*, Deepak Chopra's *The Seven Spiritual Laws of Success* (which I would have placed in spirituality) and the Joseph Campbell and Bill Moyers special *The Power of Myth* (the transcript of which was published as a book). Even Paulo Coehlo's enduring classic novel, *The Alchemist*, makes the cut (once again, a story I would align more with spirituality, even though in essence it is about self-evolution). Then there's Susan Jeffers' *Feel the Fear and Do It Anyway*, Stephen Covey's *The Seven Habits of Highly Successful People* and John Gray's *Men Are From Mars, Women Are From Venus* — you will have heard of them, perhaps even read them.

Butler-Bowdon makes the pertinent point in his introduction that because the list is generated from his own reading and research, it might be a fairly different list coming from another person. He also makes the important argument that 'the self-help ethic has been with us through the ages'. A fair comment given self-help's purview of happiness, fulfilment, dreams, transformation and power of thought. Humans have always had problems, and while you might say we have less need to fight for survival, our human behaviours haven't changed that much.

In his book *The Happiness Fantasy*, Carl Cederström posits some interesting points about self-improvement from the American perspective. Tapping into what humans desire, he says the 'happiness fantasy is a shared fantasy of the good life', bringing together moral values that, as a set, offer a 'road-map' to what can be deemed 'the happy life'.

He acknowledges the changing nature of these fantasies, citing the Greeks' preference for a life that is quiet and contemplative, and he believes the psychoanalyst Wilhelm Reich has profoundly influenced modern notions of happiness with the idea that the pursuit of authenticity could lead to a pleasurable life. Despite Reich's aggression, Cederström says he was formative in the human potential movement. Reich saw the inner potential of humans with more optimism than he did society's organisation — which he believed to be oppressive in its prevention of people becoming their true selves. 'Reich was more optimistic about humans' inner potentials than he was about the organisation of society, which, in his view, played an oppressive role, preventing individuals from becoming who they really were.'

Cederström's interest lies in 'the rich West' — 'a fantasy of self-actualisation, according to which there is only one way to become happy, and that is by reaching your full potential as a human being'.

This is the path of the individual. I think it's a valuable observation; self-help has many strands, but its beating heart is the power of self, the potential but dormant greatness that lies within you, and your right to claim it. The rest of the world — its problems, heartaches, boundaries and people — are your blockages.

The New Age approach, however, despite its elements of greed and hubris, is generally a collective consciousness experience. It is about self-improvement but so that you can be in service of others, as Marianne Williamson argued at CYL, so that you can create a better world and beautify its ugly parts.

Cederström quotes Donald Trump who, when seeking to be elected, invoked that 'Make America great again' sentiment, this time by talking about his ability to identify 'untapped potential' in business. Cederström relates this back to the 1960s, when the US was considerably invested in the world of inner exploration. That is, through psychedelic drugs and Eastern mysticism, combined with modern psychology.

This investment in human potential has not ceased. Cederström suggests it 'reflects a version of the American dream but also a vision of happiness'. He doesn't say that achieving self-actualisation is a delusion; his book is very much focused on the 1960s countercultures' 'happiness fantasy', one that grew popular in its rejection of conservatism, wealth, domination and violence.

But half a century later, the fantasy has shape-shifted. Self-actualisation is not an alternative to capitalism, it has been absorbed into it. Importantly, he sees its truly dark side, the way it teaches people to think unmercifully about failure, drenched in the notion that we are responsible for everything that happens in our lives. It has 'turned into a cruel and menacing doctrine', sustaining and normalising wealth and class difference in modern capitalist society.

THE HAPPINESS INDUSTRY

This so-called 'happiness' industry is big business. At the start of each new year, retailers latch on to the uncertainty of a frazzled, hopeful population that has made big promises to take better care of their minds, bodies and spirits. You will be flooded with emails spruiking 'New year, new you'. The problem is too much choice, and this is what can drive you to confusion — are you here to fix yourself up to be of service, or to boost your self-worth and live your best life, with buckets of money and fancy homes around the world?

Whichever voice speaks to you, don't be put off by the idea that self-help is for the weak or, on the other side of that, for the success-hungry. Advice does not equal a quick fix, but spend enough time searching through what's on offer and you will likely find potential remedies and solutions for discontent, malaise and trauma.

The *Sydney Morning Herald* reported in 2018 that in Amazon's first year of trading in Australia, self-help books were big sellers, taking up eight out of the top ten spots on the bestselling books list. Australians, it seems, are interested in books that cater to personal development. There is no denying the blended cheese of the New Age and self-help, the kind that abounds on social media, in memes about loving yourself and forgiving others. It lives in inspirational or purifying quotes misattributed to Rumi, Hafiz, Gandhi and ex-presidents. The all-you-can-eat esoteric buffet, always designed to uplift. We are more comfortable admitting that we are broken and sometimes find life hard. And we are feeling it more strongly at a time when social media showcases the #blessed life — even amid great uncertainty in a world ravaged by environmental disasters, political turmoil and, most recently, the COVID-19 pandemic. Given that self-help and the New Age tend to appeal more to women, there are also threads of sisterhood, of a rising divine feminine energy, a reclamation of the goddess spirit.

Spiritual work can encompass these things but it requires something difficult to comprehend if you don't feel it — faith, or belief in unseen forces at play in your life. And note: faith and belief are not the same thing. You can believe in God but not have faith in Him. You can have faith in some invisible, divine entity but not put a name to it because you don't know what it is.

Increasingly these spheres of influence overlap and intersect (mind, body and spirit). Despite the overlap between self-improvement and spiritual pursuit, self-help can cut itself off if it relies on self-improvement without the spiritual undertones. Ultimately, you are a participant in your own mind, body, spirit work.

Your nature and character help considerably to define how you live and see the world. You may think a few self-help books have helped you to overcome your fears but it's difficult to say that if you require systems to uphold your security. And that's what they can sometimes do. They differ in structure but dissolve into community allegiance and, once again, you are submissive and lost.

This is why so often people fall into acting out the same behaviours across different systems. The fundamentalist religious person becomes the fundamentalist vegan. The diehard self-helper becomes the New Age priestess. And this is why the New Age and self-help spaces demonstrate a full spectrum of human behaviour.

Patterns. They become more obvious and pronounced, too. Spend enough time in these spaces and you will eventually see the universal grievances, hopes and fears that form the architecture of healing modalities. The rage and depth of feeling at, say, a conscious dance gathering is palpable.

MBS is rife with potential issues — most particularly the sense that people can get locked into thinking there is always something to fix, or that their evolution is just an upgrade to the next problem and, therefore, sequel or seminar.

In self-help, there can be tendency towards self-blame. While it's an industry predicated on helping people find freedom and achieve self-love, it partly does this by making you completely responsible for what is happening in your life. External, random events are things you attracted because of your energy and thinking. I don't know that having negative thoughts is a healthy way to exist in the world; at the very least, your perceptions of life will be influenced by your state of mind. Philosopher Alan Watts supported this idea, referencing Shakespeare: 'There is nothing good or ill. It is thinking that makes it so.' What he's saying is that how we think determines how we respond to life. Fair enough.

But this idea that the universe is selective, or reflective, sending back to you only what you put out, is exhausting. Others speak of the universe's benevolence; it loves you, and you're the problem so stop being ungrateful or blind to its possibilities.

Depending on how woo woo you consider yourself, and how much you are willing to accept as plausible, you may or may not find a connection to the works of Esther and Jerry Hicks, who claim to be channelling a body of super beings called Abraham. Even if you find this difficult to stomach, the books have some useful advice, so you can't discount them completely. But it certainly posits the idea that you create your own reality and that the law of attraction is a 24/7 proposition.

Louise Hay similarly pushed a notion that we create our own realities, including physical health. In *You Can Heal Your Life*, she offers 'The List' with the affirmation: 'I am healthy, whole and complete.' The List is taken from her book *Heal Your Body*.

This idea of trapped emotions leading to physical issues is also contained in a book called *The Emotion Code* by Dr Bradley Nelson. It's kind of like kinesiology for the householder. Or what in yoga is called *samskaras* — i.e. blocked energies.

A friend of mine introduced me to Nelson's method. I found it interesting; identifying trapped or lost emotions from the past, sometimes down to the year. You use muscle testing or a sway method to identify the issues, then clear it with a magnet, literally. Being a lover of ritual, the process spoke to me.

Awareness is your most important tool. This I realise one morning as I contemplate the sheer volume of offerings available to people on a search for something — greater meaning, wholeness, prosperity. You can get caught up in a hamster wheel of action that does nothing but give the impression of progress, a pleasant feeling that falls flat when you come down from that high and didn't get the quick fix. Or you did and you immediately say, now what?

The point of any journey is to claim inner strength and fulfilment and not be reliant on external sources for happiness — said many times before Mark Manson et al.

THE 'CLASSICS' OF SELF-HELP TASTER

As you will have gathered by now, the self-help genre is not as distinct as you might expect. It has its spiritual undertones, and I've even seen books I would have thought were self-help shelved in psychology. It can help people to address issues with their bodies, but this is generally linked to the mind — otherwise it's wellbeing or wellness (think Paleo and Keto diets, and books on gut health and exercise).

Now, a lot of people will name-drop a book that changed their life, but this is particularly prevalent with self-help. Given it is all about self-improvement, it's perfectly aligned with recommendation: if something works for you, of course you will tell others about it. And if you have a spare copy you can send it to them, or perhaps recommend where to find it.

How to Win Friends and Influence People, Dale Carnegie

Dale Carnegie is like the grandfather of self-help with this ridiculously successful book, originally published in 1936. This is kind of the essential tome for the business executive (or aspiring Don Draper). It's about relationships in that it looks at how you deal with people and make friends. And it works on law of attraction ideas because it's designed to help you increase your earnings. Thrown in for good measure are some notes on how to behave, particularly when it comes to things that annoy the crap out of you or make you lose business.

You Can Heal Your Life, Louise Hay

The title itself leaves it wide open to mockery. There was a time when Louise Hay's beaming expression sent me to the cookery aisle. But then I decided to give her a chance. Hay's premise is that how we think and deal with the events and people in our lives, unsurprisingly, impacts how we feel.

The Power of Now, Eckhart Tolle

Eckhart Tolle is not on this list merely because he has a name that sounds a little mystical and witchcraft-y.

He is the author of one of the biggest self-help sellers, *The Power of Now*. You may know him also from his other work on life fulfilment, *A New Earth*. Tolle's writing is more about spiritual enlightenment. It is about 'being', about understanding that there is only now, that we are on a journey and that purpose has both inner and outer values. It is greatly aligned with Vedic tradition.

The Art of Happiness: A Handbook for Living, His Holiness the Dalai Lama and Howard C. Cutler

Personally, I think that given the way this is being sold to us — (a) that happiness is an art and (b) all you need is a handbook — this should replace all orientation material at university or in the workplace. Let's face it: if happiness is an art, most of us are screwed. I always thought it was just a feeling, but potato-potaaato. Still, this contains the wisdom of the Dalai Lama, written with more authority than the meme-friendly quotes you'll find on Facebook motivational pages.

The Secret, Rhonda Byrne

This is the book that sold to the world what Louise Hay had done years before — the way you think can change your life, and you can attract all that you desire. To put you out of your suspense, you can't achieve everything you want, but you can probably achieve a whole lot more than you think you can. For example, I'm not equipped to be a pastry chef or a chocolatier — a crushing disappointment given my particular passion for the latter's output. No amount of affirmative thinking is going to change that, unless I want to give up my day job and spend the next three years learning the ins and outs of chocolate. Still, the staggering success of the book is testament to Rhonda Byrne's ability to attract abundance.

Awaken the Giant Within, Tony Robbins

Tony Robbins' message is all about getting over yourself, using a method called neuro-linguistic programming (NLP). NLP focuses on reprogramming your mind through various techniques using psychotherapy and the like. It is a bit out there, and is sometimes described as pseudoscientific, but there is a huge amount of value in realising that we are all carrying the shards of our broken childhoods with us into adulthood. The reason why we secretly love Dr Phil is because we wish we could have him over for a lamb roast and talk about healing our inner child.

Robbins' popularity continues to grow over the years since *Awaken the Giant Within* was published. He tours the world, running days-long seminars, convincing people to walk over fire. Nowadays, he has also moved into more spiritual offerings like mala bead necklaces designed by his wife, Sage Robbins, the proceeds of which go to supporting The Tony Robbins Foundation programs.

The Seven Habits of Highly Effective People, Stephen R. Covey

One of the most famous and widely read self-help works is Stephen Covey's *Seven Habits*, which is now 30 years old. He tells us essentially to get real when it comes to dependencies and emotion, offering such nuggets as 'be proactive' and 'put first things first'. He's all about the self-mastery and should be deemed a yoda. Sure, you could argue it just makes good sense, but a lot of us don't have good sense, so paying someone $21.95 to point out the obvious is not such a bad thing.

The Mastery of Love, Don Miguel Ruiz

This book derives from Toltec wisdom, which is philosophy derived from a Mesoamerican culture. If you're wondering why personal relationships fall apart, or why finding 'The One' doesn't actually make you as happy as you thought it would, you are reminded that it's because nothing really changes and everywhere you go, you're still you.

It's sage advice, and though he wanders off into very confusing territory by the end, it doesn't discount the awesome simplicity of the rest of it. Love yourself, people.

The Power of Your Subconscious Mind, Joseph Murphy

Joseph Murphy was the original law of attraction/abundance yoda. This is old-school wisdom, written lyrically and not so drenched in the modern catchphrase-esque advice so popular in self-help. It's kind of like sitting down with a grandparent and listening to stories of ancient and modern history lore. He was a proponent (and minister) of New Thought, a nineteenth-century spiritual movement that has no single creed and emphasises the power of the mind in healing, and the idea that higher intelligence, or God, is everywhere. It does not reject modern medicine, and some commentators suggest that it's a way of thinking that shows up in the everyday motivational and transformational language of people aligned with self-improvement.

Quantum Healing, Deepak Chopra
He's the world's most famous endocrinologist, and while most of us plebeian folk have little idea of what an endocrinologist does, it sounds fancy and like the kind of work that makes him a qualified speaker on matters of the body. Anyhoo, Deepak Chopra is a guru on health matters, and is more about healing bodies than minds. However, as any self-help initiate can attest, it's all connected, and there's a commonly held thought that the way you see the world and yourself impacts your health. This means curb the worry so that it doesn't manifest itself in the form of something negative in your body. He is also wise in the ways of Vedic traditions; he studied with Maharishi Mahesh Yogi, the man who brought Vedic meditation to the west.

Feel the Fear and Do It Anyway, Susan Jeffers
The additional tagline reads: *How to Turn Your Fear and Indecision into Confidence and Action*. This may save you some time given the title pretty much delivers the entire premise of the book. However, it does contain some useful anecdotes and nuggets of advice. If you're unsure, my advice is to feel the fear and read it anyway. (Do you see what I did there?)

The Vortex, Esther and Jerry Hicks
While definitely belonging in the realm of New Age because of the method of delivery (channelling divine

beings called Abraham), this book offers the kind of advice that you might find elsewhere in mainstream self-help. The Hickses' works are all about the law of attraction, about deliberate creation and receptivity to life's gifts. You will find this in the more modern works covering the quantum field of infinite possibilities. Which brings me to . . .

Breaking the Habit of Being Yourself, Dr Joe Dispenza

Joe Dispenza gets you with common sense and science, if atoms and particles and the human brain's ability to create things is your bag. His meditations feature some challenging breathwork and trippy experiences 'in space'. His purpose is to help you recognise the habits and beliefs that negatively shape your existence so that you can create a far nicer reality. I'm not so comfortable with manifesting material gain, but there is certainly an inner journey to be found with his work if that's what you seek.

The Subtle Art of Not Giving a F*ck, Mark Manson

Mark Manson, who followed up this wildly popular book with *Everything is F*cked: A Book about Hope,* is not simply cynical about self-improvement, he's actually reworking existing ideas around it. It is not ground-breaking to advise people to surrender more in their lives. Our mythology genius Joseph Campbell told us for years about the importance of the singular pathway, of following 'bliss' rather than focusing on closed doorways. Given the confluence of self-help and New Age thought, trust and patience are easily found in books on self-improvement. Manson calls himself an 'asshole' in the book. That acidic humour is his schtick. He writes well, and he's funny, sure. But I think he's being unfair towards self-help writers who genuinely offer similar ideas, just in a less 'cool kid' kind of way. He makes it sound like the entire self-help world espouses blind positive thinking, which simply isn't true.

The Life-Changing Magic of Not Giving a F*ck, Sarah Knight

Sarah Knight does the whole no-fucks-to-give thing as well, but she manages it with more grace, even if she is similarly biting and witty about human vulnerability and folly. The title of her book, *The Life-Changing Magic of Not Giving a F**k*, sounds like a parody of Marie Kondo's *Life-Changing Magic of Tidying Up*, but it's not. It's more a salutation, a nod to how decluttering her physical life led her to declutter her mental one. Knight decided to draw up a 'fuck budget' and choose more wisely what she gives her attention to. Like Manson, she's delivered more writing on self-improvement. Her sequels are written in the same, modern style. A little self-deprecating and gently mocking, but aspirational nonetheless.

CHAPTER FOUR

Sceptics R Us

There is a group of sceptics who add content to Wikipedia, and they have a small table at Skepticon: Australian Skeptics National Convention. They are 'Guerilla Skeptics', representing the 'Guerrilla Skepticism on Wikipedia' project. 'We're targeting areas like alternative medicine, paranormal beliefs. We've got a few people — scientists — who write on religion and assisted dying,' one of them, Harald, explains, 'to make sure that people get a fully balanced view of the topic.'

With a name like 'Guerrilla Skeptics', common perceptions of sceptics grow heightened and warped in my mind; camouflage-wearing conspiracy theorists whispering into walkie talkies, but Harald and his associates are calm and amiable. Harald further demolishes the illusion by going on to say that they, quite reasonably, don't delete content they disagree with: information about magic, for example, is simply information for the masses. Rather, they try to link to scientific evidence that proves whether something is a bunch of hooey.

A woman beside him, his wife, Julie May, calmly responds to this observation. 'If we went back to the beginning of the organisation, the name would be different.'

They number around 120 people worldwide. 'And they edit in multiple languages,' Julie May says, like a tour guide.

Of course, vigilantes in favour of magic will undo their work but, these guys acknowledge, 'That's just Wikipedia'.

I venture to ask, 'If you were to define in a basic way what a sceptic is, what would it be?'

'Someone who asks questions,' Harald responds without skipping a beat.

Well, I did ask for basic. It occurs to me that there is a blanket assumption that spiritually minded people are not thinkers. And yet, while I can't speak on behalf of all, I would suggest that it's thought that leads us much of the time. Seeking, but attuned to the unseen, the mystery. Something not found in a lab, but within.

'So it's about proof.'

'Yep. Give me evidence,' he says.

'Rational thinking and evidence-based,' Julie May adds.

'Can you be spiritual and sceptical?' (Like me.)

'Yeah, there are Christians, religious people that are sceptics. Sceptical in other areas,' says Harald, though I'm not sure he's convinced.

'Everyone's got their weak points, all their vices, all that sort of thing,' continues Harald, as though he's talking about people weaning off addiction. 'So they believe what they want to believe and they find it hard to be shaken from that area, but other areas, you know, they ask a lot of questions.'

A significant part of me is preparing for a defensive vibe at Skepticon, the kind you find hardcore atheists brimming with as they tell you how deeply they don't believe in God. But Tim Mendham, executive officer of Australian Skeptics, is nothing like this — he's easygoing, friendly and agreeable. Tim is perhaps the only professional sceptic in Australia — he works in a contract position paid by a bequest of a million-and-a-half dollars made some time ago. 'They didn't love their relatives,' he jokes. 'And they hated creationists.' Fundamentalist Christians, to be more specific.

Tim explains that while there are all sorts of sceptics, the 'premise' of being one does not lie in being a cynic, or dogmatic and combative. 'It is to be someone who is seriously trying to find out what the truth is, but they're looking at it from a scientific perspective. Critical thinking is probably what sums it up the most.'

Critical thinking — something we all do, every day.

'But a sceptic is the process. The outcome might be party pooping, right? We're saying, "Sorry. That is not what is happening here". But the scepticism should be the process.'

There's a lot to debunk as a sceptic. In the book *The Skeptics' Guide to the Universe: How to Know What's Really*

Real in a World Increasingly Full of Fake, Steven Novella (with Bob Novella, Cara Santa Maria, Jay Novella and Evan Bernstein) unpacks a large world, one that pulses with a desire for reason, knowledge, truth and science. Like Tim, they favour critical thinking, and see sceptics as 'the first, and often the last, line of defence against incursions by pseudoscience'. It's their 'core area of expertise' to 'expose pseudoscience for what it is' and to help people understand the difference between it and actual science, as well as how false beliefs are formed, maintained and promoted.

Tim says we're all sceptics in a way, applying critical thinking to everyday matters.

'You buy a fridge. And you decide how big it's going to be, what brand do I get? Freezer top? Freezer bottom? What colour is it? How efficient is it? And that's applying critical thinking to that decision-making. You take evidence from different sources and you weigh it up.'

Before Tim can start talking about other home appliances, we move on to belief, because much of what concerns sceptical thinking relates to this. He says religious belief is a family inheritance. People use less critical thinking than they do buying a fridge, he adds.

I agree that we inherit beliefs and practices. And I suppose there are many people who don't unpack them, either embracing that way of life or diluting it: Christians who only go to church at Easter and Christmas (or just trade chocolate eggs and gifts under a tree); Ramadan Muslims who only fast during the holy month but otherwise don't practise; cultural Jews, who see themselves as Jewish but are not religious.

Later, I catch myself thinking about this more. And I have to say that, eventually, many of us do apply critical thinking to our beliefs. I wonder if it's possible to live a complex life in this human body, with our outstretched minds, and not question things.

I interrogated my beliefs as a teenager, at a time when my OCD was becoming a problem. To my surprise, it was something I could talk to my parents about and they didn't blow a gasket. Even now, my parents, who pray regularly, have open conversations about the nature of religion and belief.

Tim's guide to life: 'You say you can fly, and I say, "Show me". And that's it. It really is as simple as that.'

Except there's more. 'Now obviously, if you're going to fly, I'm not talking about hopping on a plane [but] under your own power, flap your arms, whatever, right? It's a pretty unusual thing. If you can fly, you would open a whole lot of new areas of research.'

What Tim worries about are New Age figureheads and their unique language. 'Basically, you get people like Deepak Chopra, who's a spiritual advisor. He throws words in without any sense of meaning. Without any sense of critical thinking at all. And they just sound impressive because he throws them in at a rapid rate.'

I find this a bit harsh. I have read a bit of Chopra, can see where the appeal in his works lie. Moreover, let's not ignore the volumes of scholarship that inform these modern New Age thinkers. But, as a self-proclaimed sceptical believer, I'm starting to see where the disconnect between spiritual pursuit and critical thinking lies. If we take, for example, experiences of transcendence, the point is to go beyond thought, not to think critically. If you are looking for an experience, this requires a level of surrender and abandoning logic. I suppose you can apply critical thinking to what is 'provable', but anyone truly pursuing spiritual fulfilment is most likely more interested in how the experience makes them feel, rather than what it proves.

But these are sceptics, and to them, proof is paramount. So they focus on debunking what they consider the vacuous, nonsensical aspects of the New Age. At the conference, there are word magnets on sale, each one a nod to the language of the New Age they find debunkable: ancient, continuum, wisdom, paradigm, cosmic, spectral and so on. I'm surprised to find placebo on the list.

'The actual evidence for a placebo is not concrete . . . That's the way science works,' says Tim, who is nice but also a buzzkill. 'Science can't be a hundred per cent sure. If you hear anyone who says they're a hundred per cent sure of something, they're not being scientific.'

'Why does it matter so much to be a hundred per cent sure? Isn't the joy of life that you don't always know?'

'Absolutely. I would totally agree with that, actually. And I think the learning is the better part, rather than the end result.'

Tim suggests that scepticism should be a conscious learning experience. 'It requires thinking. It's not about belief. Certainly not about blind faith. Or certainly shouldn't be.' He's even critical of unblinking mass devotion to sceptic 'heroes' — Richard Dawkins and the like, the atheist types who antagonise those who believe.

'Exactly,' I say. 'How is that helpful?'

'It's not helpful at all,' Tim agrees, the amiable fellow he is.

Scepticism for people is often just trying to figure something out. Tim and I consider the intrusion of logic when you have grown up with religion or spirituality. But also, the element of faith — not needing to convince others. Everything is a process, including science.

'It's not an answer, because the answer changes all the time, right?'

Scepticism with a capital 'S' is about pseudoscience and the paranormal. And, Tim notes, calling something 'pseudoscience' is not saying it's wrong, 'it's saying it's just outside of the parameters that we know now'. However, pseudoscience includes 'pseudo-medicines', treatments that claim to be medicine, but the techniques or methods or ingredients are outside what are currently known to work. Tim says the evidence on people being cured isn't there.

The main purpose of the Australian Skeptics is to address the charlatans. Tim thinks people who claim to speak with the dead are crooks and should be shut down. 'But they're so experienced in doing what they do that they avoid being tested. They don't care. They don't need endorsement from us.'

I agree that in this unregulated sphere of business, people can get hoodwinked. I have had my share of readings and know that a lot of the people doing them were inaccurate. I didn't always feel that they were knowingly terrible, though. Sometimes, people think they have some exceptional talent. Other times, people don't care, they just want to make a buck (though, outside of the superstars of the New Age, most readers aren't travelling the world and occupying mansions overlooking the ocean). And some things work in their own strange ways. Not everyone who hands over money to a healer or a psychic is an innocent being scammed, nor is everyone paying a psychic or medium some naïve victim of a scheme. There is an industry in this because people want it. Tim half-heartedly meets me halfway on this, I think, when he responds with critical thinking as a measure: 'I don't care what they think. Just think.'

He has a real beef with the use of words that are scientific sounding. 'All the time, you hear the New Age talks about energy, and vibrations, and it's so lazy,' says Tim, who argues that the word 'energy' is overused. '"Energy" is unknown to science.'

I nod along, professional and interested, but I feel a bit stung. Just quietly, 'energy' is one of my go-to words (usually invoked with like-minded people). But it's the only way I can explain what my mystical and spiritual pursuits involve — a field of 'energy' that you are a part of, can tap into and feel. You know when you meet someone and immediately don't gel? Their energy puts you off? Sure, we can't quantify it (though there are people who are doing the research); but do we need to?

While most sceptics don't believe in God, they are not like the rationalists who are interested in proving believers wrong. If someone makes a claim, it's up to them to prove it, Tim says.

I'm surprised, though, when Tim declares: 'I don't want highly rational thinking.' He doesn't like 'absolutes'.

'It's not what you expect to hear from a sceptic,' I say.

'I know. And you don't, a lot of the time.'

'Do you, just on a personal level, discount the fact that you might have intuitive abilities?'

'I've never seen any.'

'You're not operating on your gut instincts sometimes?'

'Oh, always. Everyone operates on gut instincts.'

'Then what is that?'

'But that doesn't necessarily mean you're correct. The thing is, you have experience for the world, and you're saying that, this normally works fine.'

'Have you ever had an experience, though, where, putting God aside, you had a sense of gratitude for the timing of something? Or, it was a bit woo woo, and you couldn't explain it?'

'There are certainly things that have happened that you can't explain.'

'So what does that fall under then?'

'Luck? Chance?'

Life is random. 'That's what a lot of people have trouble with,' says Tim. 'And therefore, they want some explanation for why something happens. They have to try and find a mechanism for why . . . "What happened to that person? They were a nice person. Why did this have to happen?" Well, shit happens. Unfortunately, that's the way of the world. Not pleasant. Certainly not sought after, but . . . the world doesn't care about you.'

Ouch, I think. But I don't completely disagree. We are consumed by the need to get things right. But none of us truly knows what lies beyond this human experience, in this body and with this mind. This adds a decent amount of pressure to make this life count. But what do you prioritise? A life of purpose and meaning? A life of service or solitude? An acceptance that we are creators of how our lives run or that we have little choice because life is random?

Psychics' homework

At Skepticon, Richard Saunders, a life member of Australian Skeptics and host of *The Skeptic Zone* podcast, shared some initial insights from a two-year research project on Australian psychics. Saunders collected the predictions published by psychics, seers and mystics in Australia, with the intention of 'marking their homework', and judging their accuracy.

The predictions go back years, leading Saunders to pore over the pages of women's magazines (which tend to feature psychics) along with morning television (especially around the silly season).

These predictions are usually general ones for the collective, much like a horoscope. But Saunders and his team of helpers have focused on celebrity predictions, 'by far the biggest category of psychic predictions'. People reading these magazines and watching morning television want to know about Nicole Kidman, as well as royals and politicians. 'Terrorism gets a mention especially after 9/11 . . . there's lots of natural disasters, something on the economy . . . who's going to win the Melbourne Cup . . . society in general . . . Every year a senior royal is going to pass away.' Saunders quips that there are some very senior royals, so one day this prediction will come true.

Saunders laid an exhaustive methodology, remarking that it wasn't as simple as predictions being right or wrong. 'Were they correct? Was this prediction correct but expected? Which is an important one. Was it correct but was it a 50/50 shot? Like, there are two teams in the Grand Final . . . that's a 50/50 shot. Is it just flat-out wrong? But is it wrong with a 50/50 shot? Is it too vague? And many of them . . . we could not pin down. They just waffle, and waffle, and waffle about mysteries and influences, they're simply too vague. And many are still open because we've got so many to mark.'

The psychics homework scored low across the board. In one case, only four out of 43 predictions were correct; another, three out of 71. One woman scored twelve out of 126.

'Some of these you can't mark because they talk about the personal life of celebrities,' Saunders noted, '. . . so it can be very hard to nail down.'

Still, he's made his point with what is only a preliminary report card: a golden rule of psychics seems to be to make many predictions, mostly vague, some very precise, and get something right. 'All they have to do is make one very precise prediction in their whole career which comes true, and they can dine off that for years.'

I don't know how highly people regard celebrity psychics' predictions about celebrities and politicians. However, where this matters more is in the promotion these platforms give to these psychics, who will then go on to charge hundreds of dollars sometimes for a reading.

> And there is no denying that the psychic industry works on potentials, often so vague that it would be difficult to completely reject or embrace them.

～～～

THE PALTROW SCALE

Each year, the Australian Skeptics present The Bent Spoon Award 'to the perpetrator of the most preposterous piece of paranormal or pseudoscientific piffle'. In 2018, the winner was wellness vlogger Sarah Stevenson, who blogs under 'Sarah's Day', for promoting a cure for pre-cancerous cervical dysplasia with natural products and prayer.

'She's got a million followers,' says Tim. He thinks most of them would be young women. But Tim isn't interested in punching down on those followers. It's the peddlers of these products that he believes should be addressed. We're getting along, so I'm tempted to high-five him, but instead I nod along. It's becoming clearer that the sceptics, while unimpressed by New Age beliefs and practices, are most feverish about protecting people from pseudoscientific solutions for health. I could never truly join the club; while I can be sceptical or wary at times, at heart I am a spiritual person. But I can get on board with debunking question-able, and especially dangerous, products.

In an online world of pseudoscientific celebrities, they certainly have no shortage of work to do. Years earlier, Vani Hari, the self-named 'Food Babe', was widely ridiculed for the tenuous claims she made about chemicals and food. She's been liberally debunked by doctors and scientists for her takes on toxins in food and yoga mats, imploring her huge following to be afraid of chemicals, heightening fear around ingredients that can be safely consumed. As Yvette d'Entremont notes, writing for the Gawker website, Hari's deal is to take 'innocuous ingredients', take them out of context and create fear: 'This is how Hari demonized the harmless yet hard-to-pronounce azodicarbonamide, or as she deemed it, the "yoga mat chemical", which is yes, found in yoga mats, and also in bread, specifically Subway sandwich bread, a discovery Hari bombastically trumpeted on her website.'

However, a substance can have multiple safe uses, d'Entremont adds. That includes azodicarbonamide, which you can find in a yoga mat, but also works (with FDA approval) as a dough-softening agent.

Think about the many messages you're likely to have come across spouting health and wellbeing 'solutions'. You're confronted by miracle offerings on Facebook. Upworthy-style headlines chide you for not realising the 'twenty ways coconut oil will change your life!'. You might have even subscribed to various diets that have tested your personal relationships when dining out.

Gwyneth Paltrow's Goop website has come under fire more than once for the products and services it appears to endorse. The criticism against her Netflix series, *Goop Lab*, flowed before it even aired. To be fair, some of the women's health information in the program was useful (even some of her critics agree on this), but otherwise it seems to exemplify how critics view the New Age more broadly: privileged, wealthy people wading into pseudo-science waters and spending a lot of money and time trying to become superhuman.

In 2018, the lifestyle brand settled a lawsuit for false advertising around unfounded health claims: essential oils that combat depression; and crystal yoni eggs women stick up their hoo-has. Gynaecologist Dr Jen Gunter wrote a seething blog post directed at Paltrow ('Dear Gwyneth Paltrow, I'm a GYN and your vaginal jade eggs are a bad idea'), saying it's 'the biggest load of garbage I have read on your site since vaginal steaming. It's even worse than claiming bras cause cancer. But hey, you aren't one to let facts get in the way of profiting from snake oil.'

This is where criticism is particularly important to unpacking the problem areas in woo woo offerings: vulnerable people, filled with hope or running on desperation, attempting murky solutions.

At Skepticon, Trish Hann, Clinical Educator in Diagnostic Radiology at Royal Prince Alfred Hospital and a woman with an interest in 'women's woo' leads the audience on a tour of 'nonsense health products for women', whom she says are targeted by the alternative market because women's health is linked more with lifestyle than science.

'Nonsense therapies are usually marketed as being wellness products and wellness is apparently the preventative medicine corner of the woo market,' Hann begins.

And, she says, the medical establishment doesn't take women's health as seriously as it should. Female-specific conditions are usually under-researched and new drugs are usually tested on males, even though females metabolise pharmaceuticals differently.

'So, as is the case when there's a gap in the market, businesses will often pop up to fill it and they're often welcomed with open arms by their target audience. Finally, something for me.'

Hann goes on to pillory, with good reason, several 'woo woo' offerings, awarding them 'Paltrow' ratings (in honour of her Goopiness, Gwyneth Paltrow). There's the anti-ageing Vampire Facial (because it involves your blood), which gets a Paltrow rating of four.

There are 'natural' tampons made from sea sponges. 'They're beautiful to look at, sure, but should you really be putting them in your vagina?' queries Hann. She explains that there are real risks of infection, given their porous and irregular structure. They're expensive, too, but they don't pretend to be scientific or prey on bodily insecurities, Hann says, so they only get a Paltrow rating of three.

There's natural breast enlargement (four Paltrows); vaginal chiropractic, aka gynecologic 'visceral manipulation' (four-and-a-half Paltrows); moxibustion for breech babies (four Paltrows). On vaginal steaming, Hann notes: 'The whole thing is sold as a way of connecting with your body. But there are also plenty of healing and fertility claims being made. Well, is it worth it? No. Vaginas clean themselves completely. And if you do have an infection, you'll need antibiotics, not mugwort. And if you don't have an infection, well, you might have one now because a vagina is not meant to be steam cleaned. It's not a carpet.'

Four out of five Paltrows.

The yoni vaginal eggs get a bad rating, too. Despite the lawsuit, Goop still sells the eggs, Hann says, working around those pesky false health claims by re-categorising the product. It's an 'ancient modality' or it's 'for your enjoyment'. 'So, we've got ancient, we've got science-y sounding, we've got spiritual that preyed on insecurities, it has no chemicals. I'm giving that a rating of five.'

Despite the humour, Hann's messaging has a more serious undercurrent: she urges the audience to address predatory behaviour. Hann is specifically talking about women being targeted due to their vulnerability.

'It's up to us as sceptics to educate and attack the purveyors of this nonsense, not the victims of it. We need to stop shaming women for being stupid or for being vain and we need to dismantle the structures which feed these dangerous attitudes. Take women seriously when we say we're in pain. Stop enforcing toxic stereotypes of gender or sexuality and give us an equal starting point in society.'

Hann's message is important because, increasingly, the health and wellness industries can be as dangerous as they are helpful, and like Medusa's head, full of snakes.

Shamed wellness advocate Belle Gibson may seem like old news now, but she remains an important lesson to us all. You may recall that Gibson claimed she'd suffered from a variety of major life-threatening illnesses, including terminal brain cancer, but survived due to changes in her lifestyle and diet. You may also remember that she profited off her lies, going so far as to raise money for charities that never saw a dime. She had a bestselling app, a book called *The Whole Pantry*, and a huge, hopeful Instagram following.

Initially, no one in the media seemed to query her outlandish claims of recovering from terminal illness without medical intervention. She got away with it for so long because even amid war, natural disaster and other global maladies, we want to believe that life can be restorative and kind — and, in a 'Humans of New York' era, we want to extend warmth to people who are suffering. We are also easily fooled, it seems, by an industry that is churning out miracle solutions every day. (Hint: if the words 'miracle' or 'miraculous' appear anywhere on or near a product or person, run.)

Then there's the tragic story of 'Wellness Warrior' Jess Ainscough, who actually did have cancer, and advocated the controversial Gerson therapy: a healthy lifestyle and a positive attitude to cure cancer. She wrote a book, hit the speakers' circuit and blogged about her recovery, no doubt giving hope to many cancer sufferers that there are solutions outside of traditional medicine.

While it seems Ainscough came from a place of genuine experience, ultimately she lost her battle in 2015. It's worth noting that Ainscough's mother, who also had cancer and subscribed to Gerson therapy, had also tragically died just two years before.

I have more than one friend who has been dealt the cancer card and were told of numerous solutions that would not only cure them, but also negate the need for chemotherapy or other medical attention. Thankfully, they had the common sense to consider supplemental remedies rather than reject modern medicine entirely.

It's understandable that many cancer patients, doctors and observers get frustrated by this; it's shameful to offer false hope that shark cartilage is the answer, or that crystal therapy will realign your auras and cleanse you of the negativity that gave you a tumour.

I suppose I am sympathetic to home remedies as a potential helper. My mother's kitchen cupboard was crammed with things that to an outsider's eye may have appeared little more than exotic placebo props to an ethnic household. But they never felt this way to me. Despite growing up in the West, not living in an Arab neighbourhood, and going to a school with predominantly Anglo, Greek and Asian kids, Arabic remedies were as natural as the sun rising with the start of a new day. And my mother seemed like a powerful medicine woman to me — and kind of still does, if I'm being completely honest.

Mum's apothecary comprised such things as *zayt al-baraka* (black cumin oil, aka the 'oil of abundance', to treat just about anything from a skin irritation to a cold); rosewater or orange blossom water (for gas or indigestion); tahini (throat and tummy); and olive oil (for a bunch of things including scalp issues). I found comfort in these offerings, even if at a young age I was somewhat sceptical about their efficacy. Nowadays, there is a lot more research to support the value of some of these substances (vitamins and minerals and the like).

The fact is, the search for natural remedies is as old as time. It's not that it's entirely impossible to benefit from alternative therapies. By all means, drink the herbal teas and take the tinctures if you must, but give modern medicine a chance. Where the danger lies is when they are sold as *the* solution to an illness to a person desperate for a healing.

The same can be said for all New Age practices, but especially for these closely related wellbeing 'solutions'. It's not simply a case of 'buyer beware', because some of the things you may be buying into in order to improve your mental and physical health could be adversely affecting them. So beware, but also be informed. Use your rational mind even if you favour intuition when deciding if what worked for another person could work for you.

CHAPTER FIVE

Creative Communication from Beyond

The reader closes her eyes, takes my hands and inhales deeply.

'I'm just connecting to your energy,' she intones. The sound of gentle harp music filters in from outside, a murmur of people browsing crystals, jewellery and sage sticks.

Once we're 'connected', the psychic begins to read. 'You were a queen in Egypt,' she tells me.

I play along because, why not? I'm not at the point yet where I fully appreciate what a 'good' reading looks like. And I've just dropped $60 I'm never going to see again.

'I've always felt a connection to Egypt,' I tell her, my mind flitting to a fight scene in *The Mummy*, with Brendan Fraser.

A kinesiologist once told me I had a past life in ancient Japan, where women suffered greatly. It probably sucked to be a woman in ancient Egypt, too. My thoughts travel to Cleopatra and contemplate whether the large dangly gold earrings that adorn my ears are driving my reader to make assumptions. But I'll take it, because hell yes: in my past life I was Cleopatra.

I wonder if the reader is trying to make me feel important to buffer the pain of the present. The problem isn't simply whether you believe in past lives; it's that everyone thinks they were someone important in them. This is usually what happens with past life readings: even the most ordinary life is more interesting than the present. It has gravitas to say you had it tough, or to acknowledge that you were royalty (and believe me, in group settings, this is what people do).

I'm not there to learn about a likely fictional past though. I am, sadly, enquiring about a guy who hasn't called.

Fast forward eight or nine years, and I would be married to my husband, Chris. But it would be a long road of discovery for me between then and the work I would do with psychics, readings and divination; one that would start with curiosity, become a more fervent interest, and lead me somewhere completely unexpected.

PSYCHICS AND MEDIUMS

The historically romantic view of the psychic, one frequently seen in popular culture, is the classic medium. You will find fortune tellers and those who speak to the dead in period films, coffee cup readings in Arab cinema, and tarot card readings on television. Note: seers are often portrayed as blind, in a fairly on-the-nose statement of the power of oracular sight.

Don't get me wrong: the psychic who taps into these archetypes remains; you'll find plenty who put on a show. They connect to all of your guides, angels, ascended masters, past lives, high councils in galaxies far, far aw— you get the idea. There is no denying that for many it is simply a party trick, a bit of amusement stemming from curiosity.

It's interesting then, that readers and psychics now have to place disclaimers that what they are saying is for entertainment purposes only. The new crop of readers with channels on YouTube (just look up 'Pick a card reading') state this below every video. But these are also promotional videos for their businesses, with many becoming a kind of sensation in the New Age space. I challenge you to watch a few and not get a little hooked, or to not find something that does resonate with you, even just a little. That's cosmic chemistry right there — getting that message just when you need it.

Some of the readers really know their tools, and I have admittedly lost hours to listening to them unpack stories for the 'collective' (meaning a bunch of people, not one person). If you're wanting to learn how to use tarot and oracle cards, these can offer some valuable lessons. It might also be a way to find a reader you like if you want to get a psychic reading because it's like one big cyber psychic den.

But I would be careful with using collective readings as therapy; it's not personal to you, and they are not counsellors. You could end up doing your head in with confirmation bias (where things happen that simply confirm an existing belief) or wishing for their findings to be true. After all, most of the readings are about things like twin flames (aka 'soul mates'), past lives, or when you're going to make money. You might resonate with a collective reading, but it's a bit like fast food — quick and easy, but bad for you if consumed too often.

Despite all of the scepticism directed at psychics and mediums, the industry around divination and intuition is booming. An IBISWorld report shows that in the US, the psychic services industry (card readings, palmistry, astrology, aura readings and mediumship) has seen steady growth in the five years to 2019, attributing the trend to an improved economy and 'growing acceptance of industry services among consumers'. It projected revenue upwards of $2.2 billion for that period. A Pew Research Center report on American religion in 2018 identified a trend towards New Age beliefs among both religious and non-religious Americans, noting that the majority of American adults are self-identified Christians. But the report also points out that many Christians are also subscribers to 'New Age beliefs'.

'New Age' for the purposes of the report covers 'belief in psychics, astrology, reincarnation, and the belief that spiritual energy can be contained in physical objects like trees, mountains and crystals'. As discussed in previous chapters, Pew similarly found that women tend more towards New Age beliefs than men, with seven in ten women holding at least one New Age belief, compared to only 55 per cent of men.

But first, let's talk definitions. Most people who claim to have some psychic or intuitive ability will identify with one or more of the following forms:

- clairvoyance (clear seeing);
- clairaudience (clear hearing);
- clairsentience (clear feeling); or
- claircognisance (clear knowing).

There are others, but these are the primary senses. I believe we do all have intuitive capacity, but like a muscle, it needs to be worked. And not every activity will be the ideal way to work it. The most common practices are 'channelling', where the reader is connected to guides, spirits and so on, to deliver information (they are a vessel); and using tools like cards, astrology, numerology, your palm or items you own.

Among psychics are mediums, but not all psychics communicate with the deceased. If you pay to see a medium, your session will focus on connecting to loved ones who have crossed over into the unknown. Other psychics may have that spidey sense, but they are more likely to give you a reading about you, your life and people in it.

So why do we hand over money to people to tell us about our futures or, simply, ourselves? My thoughts are that we are increasingly anxious, worried and fearful about what life can do to us, or what we think we won't have access to, whether in material form or as experience; and, frankly, from commercial advertising to social media, we're bombarded with images that project visions of an ideal life. A reading can be a prescription for hope, an affirmation of something better to come, or a confirmation that you are in a slump and have some work to do.

There is enough information supporting that this aspect of woo woo is rife with problems, like fake mediums and psychics who are simply profiting off people's despair. From my experience in this space, though, I would certainly argue that, while the industry has its problems, not everyone claiming to be a healer or psychic is a crook who just wants your money. There is potential for good.

As you have gathered by now, I'm well-versed in woo woo, and divination and intuition are where a lot of my interest bloomed into something more substantial than curiosity. But I stand by my 'sceptical believer' title, even here, as I always aim to be discerning and cautious in my approach.

I have sat with people who I believe to be intuitive, and who hate the term 'psychic' because of the pejorative connotations. I have friends who have received messages from deceased loved ones via strangers who do not work as mediums. Which is to say that I believe there is something to this, even if I also believe the industry has its share of charlatans.

This is something I discussed with two notable New Age personalities in the US: psychic mediums Colette Baron-Reid and John Holland.

A NEW KIND OF PSYCHIC

There's an interesting story of synchronicity in how I met Colette Baron-Reid, who you may remember from Chapter One. The bestselling author of numerous books and oracle decks was on my interviewee wishlist for my research into the New Age. I made some requests through her people, and when they politely declined in a 'love and light, but no' kind of way, I took it on the chin, grateful that I at least received a reply, given how frequently interview requests disappear into the ether of lost opportunities. So when I registered for her workshop at CYL with no expectation of interviewing her, synchronicity abounded when, during the workshop, we formed a connection.

At her event, Colette told us that she would be releasing a goddess oracle deck and I mentioned that I'd written a book about Arab women. She wanted to talk to me and later offered herself up to be interviewed for this book.

'When it works,' she sings. 'You asked the best questions and I thought, who is this girl?' she laughs.

She'd also seen a post I wrote on Facebook about New Age activations. These are difficult to define but they seem to involve initiating someone into an invisible energy or realm. It's the kind of thing that sends my scepticism off the charts — do we really believe someone has access to some galactic portal that can heal illness? I know I don't. Colette agreed that some of the stuff being peddled to the masses is rightly questionable.

Every week, Colette provides a reading via her YouTube channel, one that is 'prescriptive' rather than 'predictive', like a weather forecast for the week ahead; prescriptive in that she is offering suggestions on how to navigate that weather, rather than offering a fatalistic prediction of what must happen.

'So you'll know that I'm scary grounded and not telling people about their ascendance,' Colette chuckles.

Colette is definitely grounded. She's warm and engaging, with an enthusiastic laugh. You get the impression that if she's passionate about something, this is how she'll communicate — with everything, with all of her. But she's also a straight-talker, a former singer with a difficult past and oodles of funny and relatable anecdotes about her life (she calls her first marriage the 'starter husband' one). You're not going to subscribe to her list if you're interested in ascending to a crystal castle in the sky. Colette's realm is aligning with Spirit, an invisible higher force (and a common presence in New Age). When you use her card decks, you're asking Spirit for guidance. And when you're working with Spirit, you're working in that unified field to create a way forward.

Colette is realistic: there's no magic speedway to enlightenment or ongoing contentment if the internal mechanics aren't right, but oracular work is a way to tap into your intuition, and create a better life.

In her videos, Colette uses one of her decks (sometimes two) to ask what is in the air for the 'collective'. There is *The Spirit Animal Oracle* (based on her animism — the belief that all life has a presiding spirit — not indigenous culture), *Wisdom of the Oracle, The Good Tarot, The Enchanted Map Oracle* and, her most recent, *The Crystal Spirits*. Her card spreads tell 'a story in motion', so while some of them can be uplifting, and the decks are not negative, they are honest about the problems we navigate — relationships, life obstacles, purpose, health, wealth and so on.

Like a horoscope, it's a wide net Colette casts, but she encourages people to do their own readings to see what's cooking for them. She uses reversed cards, meaning she will read cards if they fall upside down — which can frighten people (reversals are generally perceived as a negative). Colette calls them protection messages (aka 'something is there to tell you how things can get better').

Colette can be troubled by semantics. 'I never used to like the word "psychic" because of the pejorative connotation of what it meant, that I was going to be Madame Zora in the corner with a turban on, somehow a fraud and taking advantage of people.'

Colette recounts how she has always received information but lacked the capacity to intuit it. After her parents died, Colette found out that her father, who taught her how to read the symbols in Turkish coffee cups, used to go into trance when he read cups, until her mother forbade it after a revelation from the grains caused trouble for a philandering neighbour.

Despite perception, Colette says she doesn't see herself as a spiritual teacher. Rather, she is a teacher of thinking, of personal transformation, of ways to make a connection to the conscious universe for the purpose of growth. Divination is an original form of such connection.

'But once you have, "I am this" — for example, "I am Muslim" or "I am Christian" — there are certain parameters and rules that go along with that immediately. If you're going to explore a more liberal [or different] way of looking at spirituality that is not determined by dogma or the confines of a structure, that people feel very safe with . . . people feel safe in the certainty of a community or group.'

Colette ponders: why do people search for answers? 'Because they're actually looking for more certainty, and they're afraid of dying.'

They want an edge on their future. This led Colette to abandon 'predictive' readings despite having a talent for seeing 'a grid of potentiality and what's likely going to happen'.

Instead, she directed her focus to asking: 'What if we could do more than what is predicted? And what if we could change and shift our consciousness and our thinking, and our story, our own personal narrative, and then see what's possible? Because we could move way past the prediction that was made, but with the prediction it would cause that person to actually see the future as fixed.'

And that is what people want, Colette says. A fixed future. Because it feels safe, even if it is not the truth. Colette created her oracle decks because she believes divination is a way to navigate our stories in motion. 'And that gives the accountability and responsibility to the person for the choices they make . . . Like, for example, how do we meet the opportunities that call us, even if they're scary?'

Oracle decks differ from tarot in terms of their structure; they are often a set of 44 cards (because four is an angelic number in the New Age), but can be any number. They can dip into mythologies old and new (Avalon, Atlantis, elementals, angels and so on). Tarot is seeing some reinterpretation in recent years, but it's generally a 78-card deck based on a major and a minor arcana (more on the arcana later in this chapter).

'I've been doing this work for 31 years full-time — *full-time* — so I went from making a living doing predictive readings then doing mediumship, which I refused to call mediumship, because I was so sceptical. I'm an openminded sceptic just like you.'

I'm surprised, but then realise what she means: like for me, some things are a big 'yes', personally confirmed over time. Other things? We'll need the data on that.

Colette's focus now is helping people to make choices and investigate their desires. With each oracle deck (she's released eleven so far), she's signalling a new way of divination: one that is less about fatalism and fate, and more about creation and finding your truth.

'Who do you want to become in this lifetime and what do you need to do in order to become that person? How do you need to change your thinking? This is what my whole Oracle School is based on,' Colette says. Co-creating reality with universal law. Recognising that you're here to fulfil a specific purpose (but not without free will and choice), understanding the difference between inspiration and want. To Colette, some things are pre-determined (typically the big stuff like when you're born and to whom), but we have choice in our lives, too.

At CYL, Colette led an intimate group in a breakout session titled 'Divine your destiny with oracle cards'. Using her own decks, Colette instructed us on how to use her cards to 'have a direct dialogue with the conscious universe'. In other words, asking for some guidance from the unseen to help unpack a current situation, what is influencing it, and where it's headed.

Colette doesn't use religious terminology; she wants her work to be accessible to all. But the 'divine' is an important component in deciphering the possibilities of your life; she interprets 'divine' as meaning that we all have a higher power that knows way more than she does.

Interestingly, despite the New Age being a space occupied primarily by women, there were a fair number of men at CYL and at Colette's seminar. I watched as one man volunteered to have his cards interpreted by Colette, and his ease listening to her (seemingly very accurate) interpretation of his current circumstances.

It was an exercise we all carried out with our own decks. Open-ended questions are best: 'What do I need to know for my highest good to create a new opportunity?'; 'How can I find a better way to work in the world?'

Colette's method of reading is explained in her weekly videos: six cards, anchored by the first one, which is the crux of the situation or messaging of the week ahead and will influence how the following cards are read. The second card offers more information and insight, followed by the others that complete the story, each one having a relationship with the others. A reading might tell you, for example, that it's important to slow down, or to be flexible with the opportunities that flow in. Colette eschews the more traditional past/present/future readings for ones that investigate the present moment and indicate the weather to come.

And in terms of her weekly prescriptive readings, Colette urges viewers to visit her website and use the online card decks for free.

In her newsletters, Colette offers her personal experiences as lessons; she talks about her own transformations and trust in Spirit. Ever present is her gentle but enthusiastic urging for people to see the power they hold to transform their own lives. Oracle cards aren't the realm of only psychics, she says; they're for everyone, a mirror, a tool for self-reflection and creative brainstorming.

The same drive informs Colette's work as a medium. It was only around seven years ago that she embraced the title of 'medium', she tells me.

I'll be honest, mediumship — a person communicating with the deceased and passing on messages — has never been my jam. I grew up two streets away from a cemetery, so I don't have an ingrained fear of graveyards, spirits or ghosts, nor have I seen one, or a jinn. But I know a lot of people who claim to have seen one and, frankly, I do believe that they saw something unusual or otherworldly. It's the story casually told that holds the greatest power for me. No one is trying to convince me, they are simply relaying an experience. Personally, I have had dreams about deceased relatives and have thought of them at random moments in a way that has left me wondering if their energy somehow remains.

Fun fact: In the Netflix show *The Movies that Made Us*, Dan Aykroyd explains that his family was way into the paranormal and that's what led him to make *Ghostbusters*.

A lot of mediums, and people in general, speak of messages being left by deceased loved ones — feathers, coins, words spoken by someone close. One woman I know, who lost her father, finds coins in her home, which she says he used to collect. A friend of mine saw a ghostly figure travel through her house soon after a friend passed away. She felt certain it was her friend coming through for a final goodbye.

But can we really channel the energy of a deceased person? I'm not sure it's impossible to connect the energy of someone living with the dead. I just don't know that it needs to be done, or if it's easy to do. Nor do I think that many people who claim to be mediums are actually speaking to the dead.

At CYL, Colette was one of the 'Three Mediums' featuring at a conference dinner alongside the UK's Lisa Williams and America's John Holland. Delegates broke bread together and watched them do their work. It was an intense experience — so many bodies and so much emotion in one small space — so I left early; but there is no denying that it's not simply 'showmanship'. The mediums on stage weren't using any tools, like cards, and they weren't walking among the attendees. Each took to the stage and did their thing, perhaps staring into their mind's eye, or hearing whispers from beyond, asking questions and seeing with whom the, at-times obscure, phrases or nicknames resonated.

One man reluctantly connected with his father. While Colette brought humour to her readings, this man was anything but happy. His father had a long death, Colette observed; yes, said the man, a well-deserved one — his father had a 'soul the size of a pin'.

No tears there.

Mediums see deceased people as spirits either in some

real visual form, or in their mind's eye. They may also feel something energetically — a presence.

Mediumship is very controversial because it goes beyond reading for someone who may just be making life enquiries. Mediumship obviously attracts people who are seeking to connect with someone who has passed on — and if it's fresh, there would be a lot of grief. Given there are a lot of fake mediums, it's easy to understand the scepticism. It can be general enough that more than one person responds to the call-out where there are numerous people; this happened a couple of times at the Three Mediums event, but only one person would end up the recipient. At other times, there were specific names or situations. The mediums didn't pretend to know if the name belonged to a person or a cat. The specificity of the names was what struck me the most.

I confess to Colette that I found the Three Mediums dinner at CYL confronting, the idea that someone's personal life can be dissected through a reading for all to witness.

'It *is* confronting,' she agrees. And it can be very personal, and intimate. 'But I have no qualms about calling myself a medium now because I know I'm doing it. There's no question that this is real.'

In her book *Psychics, Healers & Mediums: A Journalist, a Road Trip, and Voices from the Other Side*, Jenniffer Weigel shares interviews with psychics, healers and mediums. She has spent decades interviewing people who claim to have 'unusual talents'. She admits to being a sceptical journalist, but also to having an abiding curiosity about some of the head-scratching moments that keep her up at night. I sense she is like me; wondering, fascinated, wanting it to have legs.

Weigel was led into this realm of mediums, psychics and healers following a personal tragedy: the death of her father. She realised soon how 'grief is a very pricey business'.

Those last few words linger in my mind for a while. Grief certainly is a costly business, and this is where the greatest criticism of mediumship and divination lies: an unquantifiable, difficult-to-test skill that can offer a wobbly set of results. But I know lots of people who have had decent experiences, or at least readings they felt held some truth for them and therefore were ultimately valuable. The relationship to divination or mediumship is for each individual to decide.

It's unlikely that the world of magic and intuition can be regulated in its favour, but I do sense a universal shift in perception of the mystery, which Weigel also acknowledges. Saying her colleagues judge her interest in these areas, Weigel points out that humans evolve as we collect more evidence. And she believes we are seeing 'a spiritual evolution', referring to that 'collective consciousness' we covered earlier.

Weigel believes the stigma attached to mediums and psychics is less pronounced in Europe, where they're more common. And her book is an offering of examples where the truth may be more favourable to psychics, mediums and healers than mainstream New Age showcasing may allow. I have seen train wreck mediumship that was all guesswork, then I've witnessed the Three Mediums, who delivered some pertinent information for a crowd of around a thousand people.

I don't feel equipped to determine whether mediumship is hokum or not. I have no doubt, however, that there are people who have an ability to intuit messages from invisible spaces and beings — maybe even spirits who were once human. I base this on stories I have heard from ordinary people, who unexpectedly received messages from strangers.

Over the years, I have had two readings by psychics who were also mediums. One very accurately described the physical appearance of a relative who had passed away, but I didn't walk away with any knowledge beyond that. Another medium was upfront: he knew I hadn't lost a lot of people. Told me I was lucky, and I really couldn't argue with that.

My mother tells me that her own mother visited a medium when she lost her son to the civil war in Lebanon. Grief-stricken, she was hoping for connection but the medium turned her away. His death was too fresh. 'I don't want to disturb him,' she told my grandmother.

I have more in common with my mother than I initially realised. She half-heartedly studies her coffee cups over breakfast, joking about it because she's a sceptic about divination, and is devoted to God. But she likes this kind of thing. She even once, without flinching, informed my father and me that she wanted to activate her third eye. She was into readings before I ever was. But I see her catching herself, telling me something then shaking her head. 'It's all silly. Just trust in God.'

This woo woo stuff runs in my family. My uncle Mahmud, who lives in Palestine, was for a time the man you went to for divinatory advice and healings. He told me my fortune once, using my birthdate, consulting a book and quietly relaying the information back to me. It was in Arabic but I managed to keep up. I was a sad singleton, so the bit that stood out was that I would have a nice husband one day. (It would be several years before I partnered with Chris.) Alas, demand for my uncle's services grew too high and he relinquished the role of local medicine man/healer. People would have to arrange marriages without his mystical influence.

In the realm of the paranormal, my younger brother Anwar has been woken up by what he considers some kind of ghost or spirit. One day, he called me in a slight panic, having been shaken awake by a masculine figure he described as transparent. In another incident, he was awoken by someone who appeared more human-like — an old woman who was touching him. When he told her to go away, she looked disappointed, shaking her head at him as she walked away. Eventually, he told these 'spirits' in no uncertain terms, and not very politely, to leave him alone, and he hasn't experienced any strange visits since. Recently, in a random conversation about ghosts, my father told me that he saw one when he was about ten years old: a man, he said, climbing up and down a ladder in the lounge room.

It's here my scepticism is at its most elastic. It starts to feel like a gentle to-and-fro, between possibility and truth. I have encountered enough people I know and often love who have experienced strange, unquantifiable things. I have felt firsthand the power of being in a group doing ritual work, and why it's so appealing as a way to strip away emotional layers. I have no problem believing there is something to metaphysical potential. But it's a more general idea I hold to, rather than specific and devotional practices.

'I tell my audiences, "I was raised Catholic, but I respect Buddhism. I respect the Jewish faith, the Kabbalah. I try to embrace it, all of it. And I look at all religion and faith as a spoke on the wheel. Every spoke is a different faith or religion. But isn't the wheel going the same place eventually?"' Meet John Holland, a world-famous psychic medium and spiritual teacher. He's amiable, casual and has a noticeable Boston accent that I can't get enough of. He is one of the Three Mediums, alongside Colette Baron-Reid and the UK's Lisa Williams.

I sit down with John Holland the day after the dinner, his demeanour a little like a harried businessman — well, a famous one, because trying to get to a quiet place to sit and chat when people are star-struck can be a challenge. At the elevators, he introduces me to Lisa Williams, who obliges when requests for selfies from fans flow.

I mention to John that the event felt a bit heavy for me.

'A lot of people experience that because, when you're doing this work, it's a three-way communication. It's the person or the audience in front of you, it's me, the medium, and it's the spirit. And where do you think we're getting the power to do this? It's coming from you.'

I love John's casual way of discussing mediumship; like he's talking about a sandwich he made for lunch, not connecting with deceased humans and animals. He is unapologetic about it; not here to defend his occupation. He's easygoing, ready to answer anything, including occupational hazards. In his breakout session at the conference, he checked on attendees ('Guys, is anybody drained yet?') because there were a thousand-plus people 'pulling energy from each other'. People need to get some fresh air, move their bodies, drink water.

'So how do you manage it?'

'I try to step back from it. The travelling is getting more to me than the work is. Luckily, I have a dog. The dog gets me up every other day to walk, to get on my knees and play, to teach me to be present, and that's another little life that I have to take care of.'

I tell him my purpose with this exploration: for anyone to be able to read this book and to better understand the New Age and spiritual practice, but also to feel like whatever their toolkit is, it's all good so long as it's respectful. We can be individuals rather than herded into a group.

John agrees. 'Otherwise, you're looking outside for yourself.'

John is the author of numerous highly successful books and card decks. More specifically, non-traditional takes on the tarot — one called *The Psychic Tarot* and another, *The Psychic Tarot for the Heart* — which feature images people can read intuitively, without reliance on a guidebook or the usual monarchical figures. Instead, there is a focus on colours, numbers and symbols. Anything to 'spark' intuition.

'And did I get push back on that,' John tells me. He's in an industry, after all, that is as obsessed with rules and structure as any regulated business would be. Innovation isn't easily accepted.

He resisted becoming an author of tarot, but is heartened that it helps people who generally want to know the same things, especially the state of their relationships. 'That's where *The Psychic Tarot for the Heart* came from. But it's not just about lovers, it's about yourself.'

It's possible that everything John does is an effort to help people with that very thing: getting to know themselves, whether it's through progression and better understanding, or by letting go of the past, forgiving.

'I tell my students, "When you're doing this work, people's lives are in your hands. They're coming to you when they're very sensitive." I didn't know if I wanted that responsibility,' he says.

John's first book is called *Born Knowing* for a reason: he was born this way, one of five kids in an Irish-Italian Catholic family. 'I was always the different one. I was always drawn to movies on television about religion, the Virgin Mary, spirits, ghosts, magic, science. Not normal for a little boy, you know?'

John tells me he used to read cards, but following an automobile accident, psychic abilities he had pushed away returned stronger than before. Still, he resisted despite encouragement, fearful of being deemed a freak.

CREATIVE COMMUNICATION FROM BEYOND

'Instead of playing baseball with my brothers, or sports, I was home either drawing or with my head buried in a book. So I was born this way. And someone said I was very intuitive as a kid, very sensitive.'

John recounts seeing 'spirit people' in his bedroom when he was young: people with different clothes just walking through the room, whom he initially thought were coming to him in dreams.

John has queried whether his talents for the supernatural are carried on from a past life. But he won't call them 'gifts' because, he says, everyone has these abilities, some are just more aware of it.

'Did it ever frighten you?'

'No. It was part of who I was. So no. I was never frightened of it. Fascinated by it, but not frightened.'

I tell him that I know people who have 'seen' things, too. I have heard many ghost tales, stories of strange happenings that may find an explanation in science but are so much more interesting because finding evidence seems impossible. Maybe this is what we like, though: the possibilities of this unseen world, with its various beings and entities sliding into our 3D (or 5D, if you're so inclined) world.

I think of a friend who told me she had a terrifying experience with a demonic lizard that tried to suck her out of her bed while she slept. I understand that for most people this sounds insane, like it's pure imagination. As I have mentioned, I don't experience this sort of thing, but stories like this abound, both in the world of woo woo and in my personal world as someone who grew up with religion. There are people who speak of sexual experiences with spirits and jinn. Or, in a less scary fashion, feeling the presence of something unearthly that steers them away from danger.

In the case of the lizard, my friend screamed and switched on the lights. It left, she said. She was definitely awake. 'After that I put a crystal grid under my bed. It was citrine, tourmaline and quartz, I think, that sort of held me to the bed.'

It's a big claim, but I have encountered enough carefully told stories like this throughout my life that I didn't blink. Friends have told me about the rituals they do to shield themselves from spirits and invisible beings, a desire for protection that springs from otherworldly experiences.

I, like many, have my rituals, too. But it's a hard thing to talk about. I ask John about how 'psychic' is a dirty word.

'It's from the Greek *psychikos*, which means "of the soul". So it never bothered me. There were some colleagues who got nervous with the word "psychic" so they called themselves a clairvoyant. They called themselves a sensitive . . . because when you think of the word "psychic", you're going back to people with crystal balls, reading palms with flashy neon lights. Or people focus too much on television or the woo woo part of it.'

'So you're reclaiming that meaning?'

'I never disregarded it . . . I never had a problem saying I was psychic. I hid the ability because I was called weird and a freak and something's wrong with you. But psychic just means "of the soul". It's part of your soul. It's always been there.'

'What do you think people are really wanting when they come to you? I've interviewed a lot of people about this — witches, healers, psychics — and they say it's always the same thing.'

'I'm known for my mediumship now.' Previously, he offered psychic services, which he says is not strictly about the future. 'It's about your past, your present, your potential future. The future isn't set in stone. And the psychic really sits with you to basically confirm what you already know.'

For the past fifteen years or so, people have sought John out to connect with someone who has passed. And so they come in for some type of healing, to know that their loved ones are still there.

'I think if psychics have a bad reputation then, forgive me, mediums get it much worse.'

I wonder how he feels about that, but John says mediumship is more common now. His focus is on being an efficient medium: 'You need proper training to do this. Not just because people's lives are in your hands. You need to know the mechanics of how this ability works so it doesn't burn you out. Because you're a physical being and a spiritual being.'

'So, what would you tell people who want to be a part of this world but are afraid or they reject it because of the charlatans?'

'I'm so used to it,' John says, who adds that he's thick-skinned, growing up a 'street kid', but also because he has two decades' experience in mediumship.

John differentiates between a sceptic ('show me') and a cynic. 'Your mother could appear right in front of them. They'll call it a holographic 3D image just being beamed in through the vent. That can't be real.' He reckons there were sceptics in the thousand-strong crowd at the Three Mediums event the night before. 'All I can do is my job and give the best evidence possible to show you that your loved one has passed away.' Not fearing sceptics means he can help the people who need it. 'Luckily I have a good reputation. I'm approachable.'

John says he's done his job if a sceptic or a cynic sees him work and leaves with questions about what they saw. 'Then maybe I opened a door for them to think that there is a possibility that the afterlife is real . . . I can only ignite it a little.'

Colette Baron-Reid addresses this with me, too. Colette believes 'mediumship can be an epiphany'. 'In that moment, that person's life has changed forever. The person on the other side wants him to heal, wants to set them free.'

She mentions the man at the Three Mediums dinner who openly shared his hatred of his father. Colette asserted, 'You loved your dad,' and he ultimately agreed. 'That made him very uncomfortable, but it changed him.'

I can't deny this. I watched from afar as the man shifted throughout the reading. Always soft-spoken, but he went from hard and angry to vulnerable.

At a party months later, my friends and I get talking. One mentions she had seen a medium recently who was on point — she described my friend's recently deceased mother's character, and how she had lived. My friend was managing well, but she was curious, nothing more. Other friends, none of them religious or spiritual, shared their experiences with mediums. One was in the crowd for a medium event at a New Age festival and received a reading of chilling accuracy. One of those 'she knew names and events she could not have known' type experiences, which my friend found comforting (and interesting).

I wondered about all of this later. About the strength of human connection, emotions that run so deep that even death can't sever them.

DIVINATION

For years, I've been fascinated by divination, which is the practice of seeking knowledge or insight into future events, taking a supernatural approach. I would say divination is popularly considered as being within the realm of 'fortune-telling', but in a modern context has shifted its co-ordinates. This is how I have found myself drawn to it: seeking insight into the future in order to have hope or find direction, but nowadays it's more a desire to better understand the present. And, as is the case for many people, it is a fascination that was born when I needed a sense that my life would improve.

I first became drawn to it when Hannah — a friend of my brother Alex and his wife Kelly — read my tarot cards about fifteen years ago. I'd never felt compelled to get a reading before that, despite friends going to psychic readers and swearing by them, and various hints that my mother, whom I consider to be deeply intuitive, had snuck in a reading or two at the Mind Body Spirit Festival. I was completely sceptical about any kind of 'fortune-telling', but I was ultimately receptive to it because, as might be the case for many, I needed some gentle assurance that life would get better at a challenging time.

Hannah read for a few of us at the dinner table, and she seemed eerily accurate to me. I watched as she carefully removed an ageing *Rider-Waite* tarot deck from its purple cloth. It looked well used, a bit romantic in its creased, browning state. The deck is arguably the most well-known and popular deck used today, first published in 1909, with vibrant illustrations by Pamela Colman Smith and words from the mystic A. E. Waite. Many tarot decks offer variations on it.

Hannah asked me to shuffle them with my query in mind, and I watched, my heart in my throat because I felt like it was a significant moment. I was so desperately hopeful for some brightness in my life.

I remember the gist of the reading: after a dark time, things will get better, and Hannah knew without any input from me that it had to do with disappointment about something that had not worked out. I think one of the cards representing heartbreak featured (three swords piercing a red heart), but it was the Six of Swords that I remember to this day: a woman sits hunched and defeated in a boat as a man rows her away, six swords planted in the wood in front of her. She is filled with sorrow but the worst is behind her. She hasn't forgotten (the swords are still there), but she is moving forward.

At the time, I was nursing a broken heart, feeling utterly lost and directionless. I knew only that I had to forge a new pathway for myself.

This card, the Six of Swords, is one of the 56 that comprise what is called the 'minor arcana' in tarot. I think of these as the everyday things, which are unpacked through four suits: cups (emotions/love), swords (intellect/focus), wands (career/work) and pentacles (wealth in all its forms). The major arcana is made up of 22 cards that tell a much bigger story, a hero's journey of sorts that starts with The Fool setting out on an adventure and ending with The World, which symbolises liberation. When you read and see a lot of major arcana cards, this would suggest major life changes are on their way.

Hannah's reading was like a massive exhalation. I felt understood, or perhaps simply reassured. It gave me a necessary prompt to find my energy and start anew. But how had she known about things I hadn't told her?

It had always just seemed like luck to me, but over the years I have grown to rather like the tarot and its winding pathways through the human psyche, its recognition of the very universal experiences of being human.

And that first reading unlocked something deep inside of me: a hunger to understand how we can change our lives, and how much fate runs the show.

When I told a friend at work about it, she shared with me her own adventures in tarot. Her deck of choice was the *Thoth Tarot*, the work of artist Lady Frieda Harris and occultist magician Aleister Crowley. The deck was a gift, she told me. 'You're not supposed to buy your own.'

My friend read for me, allowing the cards to fall upright or reversed, the latter seen as negative because it can point to a blockage or delays. For example, a card signalling liberation and joy would, when upside down, be telling you that this is not yet possible. She hinted at changes within me that I was not ready for: a relaxing of religion, more meaningful connections and a change in career. The reading was expansive, not a party trick. I saw my world break open through her eyes and my gut told me in which direction I needed to head.

I was hooked, encouraged by how cards could help you to see your situation from a fresh perspective and with hope. I was a newbie, though, feeling stuck and uncertain about my life, so I was one of those people hungry for predictive assurances. I wanted to know that good things were coming. I was yet to understand how important I was in making a better future my reality through my present actions.

Soon after, seeing my fresh curiosity and enthusiasm, my brother Alex bought me a beginner's tarot deck, *Simply Tarot* by Amanda Hall. 'Just promise me you won't become obsessed with it,' he said and I solemnly told him that I wouldn't.

Obviously, life had other plans because, fifteen years or so later, I'm writing about it.

I find the tarot an enthralling journey; I like how so many decks reflect how people live and experience life differently. Increasingly, tarot decks are more diverse and artistic. There are tarot decks featuring mythical creatures, animals, the earth, tattoo art, the circus and history, to name just a few themes. A favourite example is the *Next World Tarot*, written and illustrated by Cristy C. Road — a beautifully rendered deck that offers genuine diversity. With new takes on the traditional archetypes, Road envisions a world where power and potential lie not only in those with privilege, wealth and white skin. Her cards centre minorities across culture, religion, colour, bodies and more. She signs off in the book with 'love and rage', because the deck doesn't simply target personal transformation, but our places in the world and dismantling oppressive structures.

I've also found that some oracle decks can be useful as creative mechanisms. Oracle decks are more spacious explorations; they are often more optimistic in that, while they will address hardship, they tend to be clearly solutions-oriented. Oracle cards are generally softer, gentler methods of guidance and advice. They are good for daily use, for affirming positive thoughts and intentions for the day/week/month ahead. That's not to say they aren't truthful about the hard parts in life; the New Age is as much about our shadow sides as our light. But they're easier to read than tarot, which requires a greater intuitive interpretation and can rely more heavily on symbolism and its metaphysical limbs — astrology, the elements, archetypes and so on.

Australia's own Alana Fairchild is increasingly a big name in the world of oracular insight. She has sixteen decks at my last count (not including pocket editions and app versions for your phone), as well as numerous books that tap into the invisible in a wide-reaching way. Her decks call on the mythologies of Isis and Kuan Yin, of the mystic poet Rumi, of angels and ascended masters. Her latest deck, *The White Light Oracle*, featuring the artwork of A. Andrew Gonzalez, incorporates sound frequencies. Her latest book is called *Crystal Stars 11.11: Crystalline Activations with the Stellar Light Codes*.

I have studied with Alana, and she has the sort of energy and beaming smile that invites you into her world of communication with divine guides. My scepticism and discomfort with the grandiosity of the New Age means I'm selective about such offerings. I am always curious, but I have limits. For example, I'm not sure what to make of crystalline activations.

Can the lessons around something still have value, whether or not it's true? Yes. In the same way a fictional story can help us to realise truths about ourselves.

And while there are deck authors like Alana who clearly go deep in the creation of their cards, oracles often have one-word card meanings, like 'Love', 'Adventure', 'Release', etc. They vary in tone and focus — from nature, to elementals, to crystals, to saints and mystics. Mythological deities and creatures are popular, as are legends (King Arthur, Camelot, Avalon, Atlantis and so on). You've got fractals and sacred geometry. I find Cheryl Lee Harnish's fractal card decks quite beautiful, and can be read as simply or complexly as you wish. (You can see how she uses them in readings on her YouTube channel.) Even musician Brian Eno has a deck of sorts, *Oblique Strategies*, co-authored with Peter Schmidt, which offers abstract suggestions to cure creative block. Eno's deck is simple — black print on white cards — but most oracle decks are as much about the artwork as the narrative, and individual cards can be read on their own.

In the guidebook to the oracle deck *Divination of the Ancients*, Barbara Meiklejohn-Free and Flavia Kate Peters give a nod to a 'golden age' of wisdom and truth, of learning from 'wise ones' — that is, oracles who communicated with the invisible beings and nature, and offered interpretations of signs or omens. The deck by Meiklejohn-Free and

Peters works like any typical oracle deck — you shuffle cards and interpret them based on where they land in a spread; but it's interesting for the information it provides. Each of the 45 cards is a divination tool, and covers a wide array of divinatory mechanisms with messages attached. They note that the word 'divination' derives from the Latin *divinare* — 'to foresee', 'to be inspired by the gods'. Signs are around us daily; diviners, oracles and seers 'saw everything as a message from the world of spirit'.

History has not always been kind to the once-revered messengers of spirit. As Meiklejohn-Free and Peters note, fear changed their relevance and influence, with religious clergy replacing the shamanic oracles. It's still illegal to partake in divination in some parts of the world, while Abrahamic faiths, despite an acceptance of magic, generally frown upon or outright forbid any practice that resonates with the occult (which incidentally derives from the Latin *occultus*, meaning 'hidden' or 'secret').

Interestingly, playing cards (used for a form of divination called cartomancy) emerged from the Arab world, later embraced in the West. Both playing cards and tarot have roots in Egyptian Mamluk cards; the suits of traditional tarot are based on patterns found in the Topkapi card deck from the Mamluk era in Egypt — that is, cups, swords, coins and wands (polo sticks in the Topkapi deck). Because Islam forbids drawing humans, the Topkapi deck features Islamic calligraphy, but has a king and deputies who are not depicted.

Tarot and gypsy cards are divination tools that go back centuries. Oracle cards are a fairly recent innovation, but tarot has existed for much longer, often regarded as parlour entertainment. Gypsy cards fall under cartomancy (using playing cards) as a fortune-telling tool. Lenormand and Kipper cards are used a lot nowadays, too, but arguably tarot remains the most popular.

In recent years, the world of tarot and oracles has exploded into a proper commercial enterprise. You can find cards for any type of personality or interest. There are decks that are soft and reassuring, ones that are more brutal in getting you to a place of acceptance. There are the ones that tap into the rising every-woman-is-a-goddess mindset. There are cards for the 'starseeds' (people who feel like they're alien to the human world sometimes), 'earth angels', 'lightworkers' and more fancy otherworldly titles. All fine to work with, but not your best bet if it makes you cringe. Cards rely on you and what you bring to them, more than you rely on them.

All of these, though, for whichever aspect of you they tap into, are meant to help with an inner journey, not merely an external one. While I don't believe every thought dictates how your life pans out, I do see the undeniable interplay between how we exist inside and the external world we live in.

Beyond the tarot and oracle decks, popular tools include any other manner of cards, pendulums, tea leaves, coffee grains and palms. You can consult the stars and planets through astrology, use jewellery (psychometry), numbers (numerology) or stones (lithomancy). The Chinese have *I Ching*, an ancient Chinese divination text; the Norse their runes, which was actually their first written language.

Scrying is also done by the more advanced, in various forms: this involves using a crystal ball, melted candle wax in a ball, fire or mirrors to 'see' future events.

But, as I've discovered, you can read anything. Energy intuitive Denise Jarvie told me in an interview for *SBS Life* in 2016, 'You can read anything if you want to, from the clouds to the spoon you stir your cup of coffee or tea with.'

Insight facilitator Kerstin Fehn agreed: 'I've used sugar sticks at a café and let them drop onto the table . . . You can use a kaleidoscope. Watch clouds form. You can use anything as a reflective device.'

A fellow improv theatre student, Chris Winspear, picking up on my interest in woo woo, once told me that he happened upon a method of reading ordinary playing cards one drunken night. Meanings just came to him; he retained the knowledge and to this day still reads them. But he doesn't overwork the significance of it. Reading cards isn't about offering definitive prescriptions on fate.

'It's about giving advice,' he says. General sort of advice that can be interpreted in more than one way. 'It's not specific enough to be like, "You're going to get run over by a blue bus next Tuesday." It's more like music that'll be playing in your life in the next six months. And so learn these dance moves so it'll go well.'

More than a cup of coffee

A popular method of divining information about someone's life is to read coffee grounds or tea leaves in a cup. Mediterranean people use thick, sludgy, very strong coffee that ends up muddy, leaving imagery to be deciphered.

At the end of the reading, you can lick your index finger or thumb and stamp the bottom of the cup for any final messages. But, and this is something my mother and I do, you can also read the shapes in the coffee foam on barista-made coffee. It works the same way.

Otherwise, there is a bit of ceremony to it, as is the case with tea-leaf readings, which involve ritual (for example, pointing the handle of the cup towards your heart). Whatever the liquid, the cup will decide what you need to know.

Such readings are ultimately high on symbolism, charting a story about that person's life. You can decipher people, animals and pathways. You can build a story or a journey in a single cup, or it may tell you a variety of things — influences, warnings, assurances and energies.

There are other ways to get 'information' that don't require physical tools. Dreams can be used for divination, but they are hit and miss. They tend to arrive unbidden (though some say that praying for guidance, if done with some embellishments, will deliver a nocturnal verdict that plays out like a movie). And yet, dreams are drenched in symbolism; in the same way no one can really explain déjà vu, dreams are interpreted in a variety of ways. My mother once had a dream that I opened my hand to reveal money that was torn and dirty. The next day, the business I worked for was placed under administration and we were all let go without pay. I once had a dream about a friend standing in my house, refusing to leave. She woke me up the next day with a phone call to tell me she'd left home. I don't make a big deal of such synchronicities; I just find them fascinating. They can also be frustrating — what is the point of a dream giving me a warning shot if I can't decipher its meaning, or avoid the thing it's warning me against? I delight more in the ones that signal something positive is about to happen.

Similarly, channelling is generally done without the use of any props or tools. The issue with channelling is that it can be so general to the point of silliness (insert sceptical emoji). It can be performative and so broad that it could apply to a whole bunch of people (in the same way collective readings will not seamlessly land for all watching). One woman I requested a reading from emailed me an in-depth response to three questions, but because she delivered it late, she asked my guides for a twelve-month forecast in addition to answering the questions; it was specific and erroneous.

I also attended a session with a woman who channels; she didn't use any oracle or tarot cards, or read a crystal or item of jewellery. She asked me if there was anything I wanted to know about but before I could reply, she suddenly blurted out a few sentences about my life and personality. Then she seemed to fizzle out, unsure of what to tell me for the remaining twenty minutes.

Of course, being a creative who can write for hours in what feels like a trance mode, I don't wish to suggest that any form of channelling is impossible. We're always downloading things, which is why I'm a firm believer that we all have intuitive abilities. The degree to which we use them depends on our scepticism. Your own sixth sense is your greatest asset. It will tell you when someone is sharing information that you need to pay attention to. Good readers are a partner, helping you to figure things out. But they're not therapists, and shouldn't be regarded as such.

Still, I long ago stopped using divination readings as quick-fix emblems of hope or relief. I have renegotiated my relationship with these mystical delights. I don't consult cards, or people who use them, to acquire a template for the future. In any reading, I often have to resist the instinct to read the cards myself, which is why I will opt for a deck I have never seen or used. At some point, I learned to trust my intuition more than random readers. I like synchronicity and what I call 'energy work'; I am open to receiving signs and messages. And personally, I use cards creatively, as a prompt, to get my mind flowing, to separate thoughts and identify problems and solutions. And sometimes it's just a bit of fun with friends.

Advice from the front line

When I was bit younger, new to readings and more timid about what they meant, I was malleable and, I think, a bit lazy. I was what so many readers have described to me: someone who wanted a quick fix, to feel better about something but not necessarily work towards creating a better life for themselves. Those people are the ones keeping psychic hotlines profitable. They just want to be told everything will get better. That they will find love, make more money, and lose the weight. They are only interested in what they want to hear.

I distinctly recall a brief reading I had with a woman who told me things about myself, but nothing I wanted to hear. I was hungry for a more interesting life, and I was lonely. She told me that I should start dancing, that I would be on the front page of a newspaper, that there was much to explore in my life. At the time, I wasn't having any of it, but she'd been right on every count. Years later, I met her again and apologised for judging her so harshly. She was taken aback but smiled warmly in response. 'Thank you for saying that. But I understand that we get where we need to go when we get there.' This is important in readings: understanding the potential for information overload, or for seeing someone's possibilities in a way that advances them too far from where they are now.

I have had my share of readings, and there are a few things that stand out as being common to several of them, which I would say have a level of truth to them:

- I would become successful and well known in what I do at 38.
- I would eventually marry someone (Is it a problem if he's not Arab and Muslim? Don't worry, he's a good guy!).
- I want my freedom.
- My talents lie in communication/creative work.
- I have self-esteem issues.
- I would move out of home.

As part of my journey with research into New Age practices, I decided to approach readings more clinically, much like sceptic Richard Saunders, whom we met in Chapter Four, and who has been undertaking a methodical investigation of psychic and medium claims in popular media. I was able to come at it as a different person; I had less skin in the game, and I had become more interested in an authentic journey that would lead to a life of greater purpose and meaning. In terms of where I was at in life, I was dealing with great change: friendships I once cherished had fallen away; beliefs that once held me together like glue were melting into obscurity; and a desire to be a creative explorer, to be someone who experiences life, rather than has the appearance of an ideal one, was taking hold in an unshakeable way. I understood that something was amiss and I needed to figure things out for myself.

So I began to get readings, things I wouldn't ordinarily do, like a phone reading, a palm reading, numerology. When readers delivered very determinist and fate-based predictions, I was less interested in what they had to say. But the more observational comments about the challenges I faced as a writer with a desire to do more — to expand my creative capacities and to have authentic and loving relationships in my life — stayed with me.

The things that the readings led me to reflect on were:

- I am prone to feeling helpless if I can't help someone with their problems.
- It helps no one to hold myself back.
- Shifting focus isn't a bad thing.
- A period of destruction can precede one of construction.

The stuff I am cautious about, if not outright disinterested in, includes:

- Yes, I am a woman but it doesn't mean I want five children, so stop putting them onto me.

- I don't want health advice — swinging a pendulum to identify my vitamin deficiencies isn't my thing.
- I don't need to be lectured on how I feel about myself.
- Not everybody is well-versed in astrology — readings shouldn't depend on your knowledge of everyone's star signs (i.e. it's not helpful to say, 'There is a guy doing so-and-so, and he is an Air sign').

The vague stuff that could be a sign of psychic ability or just luck because it's common includes:

- I want to make a difference, to reach people.
- I am creative.
- I hold myself back and need to trust more.
- I am very self-aware and intuitive. (In other words, I don't really need readings.)

Based on my research and personal experience, here are some questions to ask to ensure you are getting what you paid for, and that the reader is actually offering something of value:

- Are they just studying you and making reasonable guesses about your character and situation based on that?
- Are they waiting for affirmations from you for every question, and therefore just guessing and trying to land somewhere true?
- Is what they're saying so general that, yes, it could be true, but it could be true for anyone?
- Are they forcefully telling you a future that you know in

your gut is unlikely? Readings should not be too futur-istic. You wouldn't get a second-grader to do year 12 maths, would you?

- Are they using the typical psychic phrases you hear: someone is tall, dark and handsome; you will travel over water; I see a three — could be three days, weeks or months. Not hugely helpful.

The main thing is always to feel safe and not judged. Like all things in life, take what is useful and discard the rest. Be aware that, with readings of any kind, there is the danger that you may start to negotiate with yourself. You may work something up to be true that you initially thought was bullshit; you may discard your own reason and capacity to grow, and allow the reading to influence your circumstances. Do not be at the mercy of a reader. If 'energy' is truly involved in all of this, you are dealing with the reader's, too, who may be projecting their own stuff onto you.

On a final note, please do not be afraid to look at what might be more useful for you in times of difficulty or distress. No matter how interesting, reassuring or nice a reader and their interpretation of your life is, it is no substitute for professional counselling or treatment.

CHAPTER SIX

A World of Magic & Manifestation

There is a beautiful magic shop in Melbourne. It has a large wheel of stars that you can spin to land on an answer based on the major arcana of the tarot (the 22 cards that represent milestones on a personal journey to liberation — as discussed in Chapter Five). It smells of incense and is lined with shelves of objects that seem to belong in another time. My friend Helen and I go in after a lunch catch-up. She wants to buy me a gift as a thank you for something. Even though she's a cynical, jaded Marxist who doesn't mind her tarot cards being read but thinks religion is fantasy, she knows that in this respect we are not the same.

Helen calls out to one of the women in the store to assist. She wants to know what she can buy me even though I am standing right beside her. A candle, the woman suggests. She points out one, dedicated to attaining confidence and power. Helen sniffs at the suggestion. The woman tries again: how about one for love? Seeing me (at the time) as a sad singleton, Helen leaps on it. 'Yes! That's the one.'

I accept the gift. I burn the candle down. A few other changes in me are brewing, spiritual and otherwise. Soon after, my relationship with a friend, Chris, changes tone and we fall for each other. A year and a half later we are married.

I really should thank Helen for that candle.

While I'm not a practising witch or magician, I've relished learning about these traditions through good friends who are both knowledgeable and openminded. In this chapter, two of my most trusted guides, Stacey Demarco and Christian Read, give us peeks into these realms of possibility.

WITCHCRAFT

Witches have been experiencing a really bad PR day for the last 2000 years, jokes Stacey Demarco, aka 'The Modern Witch', bestselling author, and former judge on Channel 7's *The One* alongside sceptic Richard Saunders. The show tested the psychic abilities of people claiming to have them. 'Richard Saunders and I were never more than one point different in rating people. So Richard and I had very similar opinions on people,' Stacey tells me.

Stacey knows something about the importance of PR given she was once a corporate high flyer, doing PR and marketing for Sony. 'I was a corporate animal, man,' she says with a laugh. 'I used to travel with Michael Jackson.'

I've known Stacey a few years now. She's effusive, energetic and a straight-talker. I first met her at the Mind

Body Spirit Festival in Sydney where she had a stall. She has card decks and that day was offering readings and selling talismans with particular meanings. I was intrigued but also attracted to how she held the space. She was dressed elegantly (she doesn't do the purple tie-dye), cutting a professional but friendly presence. Soon after, I began attending her monthly moon meditations, which she calls 'storytelling for adults', an expression clearly designed to make people like me — not into moon cycles, not a pagan or a witch — more comfortable. I'm a creative, so I felt the pull of a ritual that draws on mythos. Through the meditations, we would plant seeds of intention, make a wish or three, or banish what we no longer needed. I loved Stacey's passion for the stories she told, the way she carried her truth at a time when I was searching for my own.

Witchcraft is actually a common practice throughout the world. Australia's community numbers between 60,000 and 100,000. 'We are over-represented in the military, in the helping professions,' Stacey notes.

Not all pagans are witches, nor are they necessarily polytheistic like Stacey, who works with deities across many mythologies. In her pursuit of witchcraft, she trained as an Artemistic priestess, finding teachers to help her along the way. This means Stacey's patron is the goddess Artemis, a huntress and protector of nature and the earth.

There are many ways to discover the breadth and depth of witchcraft. There are books aplenty that deal in the rich history of witches around the world; the different pathways of witchcraft from the traditions of Wicca to Stacey's pagan approach.

Witchcraft is linked heavily to the natural cycles and seasons of life; to an experience of communion with the earth and its elements, and for some, to deities and beings from beyond the earthly realm. In *Earth, Air, Fire & Water: More Techniques of Natural Magic*, Scott Cunningham lures the reader into what he calls 'the true realm of magic' — not a world of curses and dark ritual; rather, the kind of magic that is more tangible and felt, calling on natural energies and love, with a trust in positive change being the result.

It's a nice reminder that witchcraft is, like most mystical pursuits, about creating change within ourselves and the world around us.

It is about unseen worlds within and without. It is as old as humans, whose religious practices in ancient times would more closely resemble magic today. As Susan Greenwood notes in *The Encyclopedia of Magic & Witch-craft*, magical tradition that 'recognises a shamanistic inter-connectedness of spirit' infuses most cultures, or has at some point in history.

Greenwood says the rise of the Christian church in Europe changed the presence of magic in daily life; magic, sorcery and witchcraft were met with a reasonable amount of tolerance until major religions made it a fearsome practice. Consider, for example, the rise of the 'evil witch' stereotype, with executions common in the 1400s onwards.

Interestingly, as Stacey tells me, the stigma is not completely erased. 'It was only in 2005 that the anti-witchcraft laws in this country were repealed. It's scary, right?' More specifically, Victoria repealed its anti-witchcraft laws in the 2005 *Vagrancy Act*. Other states either didn't have comparable laws or repealed their anti-witchcraft laws earlier (e.g. The UK's *Witchcraft Act* of 1735, which applied in NSW until 1969).

The judgement is strong enough that Stacey is careful about sharing her life path with strangers when travelling abroad, something she does quite a lot, both solo and leading sacred retreats.

Initially, this surprises me. But then, in a world where opinions are so loudly and liberally shared, such a label would immediately create a divide. 'I've never hidden away from the word "witch" . . . but in some places, for my own safety, I would say, when people say, "What do you do?" I'm an author. "And what do you write about?" I write about mythology and ancient paganism.'

It's not a lie. Stacey writes about mythology, paganism, ancient religions, deities and nature.

She is a busy woman — she writes books and oracle decks, she advocates for animals and the environment, she runs retreats and courses, and she consults with clients by distance, prescribing spells or giving readings. (Her clients, she says, have varying beliefs — from monotheistic to atheistic.)

Despite all of this, she seems well, *normal*. That is to say, grounded, efficient and not at all dressed how popular culture would have you think she should. While the word 'witch' connotes darkness and mystery (à la Salem witch trials), or a romantic vision (like a scene out of *Beautiful Creatures*), Stacey emphasises that those who practice witchcraft are typically much more conventional.

These misconceptions stem from traditional understandings of the term 'witch'. Stacey has worked hard to take the sting out of the word, refusing to go by a more exotic tag such as 'priestess' when it comes to her public profile. She's no 'white witch' either — to call herself one would be to suggest that the default is something dark. It reminds me of how often Muslims are labelled according to a spectrum — moderate or extreme. Most will tell you that they are neither.

'I'm someone who, from the moment I came out of the broom closet, I decided that I wasn't going to hide from the word "witch". People still use that word as an insult, as something disgusting . . . I want to bring honour back to it, because the word "witch" meant weaver. It meant wise person.' Witches have always been catalysts for change, she adds. 'For me, my purpose in life is to be a catalyst for change, in lots of ways.'

Silver RavenWolf, in the book *To Light a Sacred Flame*, similarly presents a focus on transformation through 'practical, magickal [sic] living' that not only leads to fulfilment of desires but also allows you to help other people 'in a quiet, meaningful manner'.

Modern witchcraft is a rich universe that does not detach from its storied history. Witch and author Lucy Cavendish, for example, dedicates an entire book to 'the occult's greatest legends' in *Witches and Wizards*. Inside, she introduces a world that she warns is not one of fantasy. Nor are its witches and wizards, who — no matter their power — are very human.

Cavendish journeys as far back as the Dark Ages in tracing the birth of magic. She offers a history of Merlin of King Arthur's court, whom she believes was a Druid. Druids were wise, reading the world around them from the stars to stones, and animals in between. They viewed them all as sacred and sought to protect them.

In *The Occult, Witchcraft & Magic: An Illustrated History*, Christopher Dell notes witchcraft's connection to shamanism, in that it saw 'special powers' being used by practitioners 'for the benefit of their community'.

Dell dates the 'traditional Western image' of witches from the time of their persecution around the fourteenth and fifteenth centuries. Before that, both male and female witches were scattered across Europe, offering 'a mixture of healing, medicine, knowledge of herbs, amulets and protection against harmful forces'.

You will find the modern witches of today are as interesting. Even Australia has a rich witchcraft history, with one of the most notorious being the 'Witch of Kings Cross' Rosaleen Norton, an artist famous for her arched eyebrows whom tabloid papers loved to feature. A *National Geographic* article by Cassie Crofts in 2016 notes that Norton's worship and artistry of the god Pan was mistaken for Satan. She was charged with obscenity multiple times.

Crofts quotes Marguerite Johnson, an associate professor at The University of Newcastle, who has long had a fascination with Norton. Johnson notes that at a very morally conservative time in Australia (1940s and 1950s), Norton was a radical, open about being a witch. She would wear men's clothing, smoke in public, live with men. She was independent.

Crofts goes on to observe that Norton's magic approach was not one of 'black' or 'white' magic. Rather, she viewed magic as 'a force and power above morality'.

There's more: sex magic within Norton's coven (she was bisexual, and apparently enjoyed bondage and sadomasochism), learned from Aleister Crowley's teachings. Crowley was infamously considered a 'black magician', whose work in magic rebelled against organised religion.

Not every witch has such an illustrious history. Nowadays, you can find them more freely, and while they are still often harassed for their beliefs and practices, the online space and a globalised community have arguably made more room for a variety of mystical and magical practices.

Bookstores are well stocked on witchcraft and other aspects of the occult and magic; oracle and tarot cards are major sellers, ubiquitous and not so dark; and you need not look further than YouTube to find witches by the truckload — channels dedicated to oracle readings, spells, how to perform chaos magic, and some things I truly wonder about, like revenge spells and other things too mean and dark for this generally interested explorer. In the real world, a retreat to find your inner goddess, or connect to a mythical one, is never too far away. Goddess circles, where women gather to ritualise, share and honour goddess energy, are an increasingly common practice, carried out by women who want to change the world, but first themselves.

It's getting popular, this goddess trend. Actress Jenna Dewan, post-divorce from heartthrob actor Channing Tatum, opened up to *Harper's Bazaar* about life post-separation in a way that pointed to her LA-inspired New Age influences. The author of the piece, Margaret Wappler, leans into Dewan's way of life, fluent herself in this contemporary age of feminine empowerment through 'everyday witchcraft', astrology and spiritual awareness. Dewan says she runs a goddess circle with women friends — an opportunity to not only make some intentions and converse, but also experience a shaman-led meditation that involves sound bowls and crystals.

LA is certainly a hub for all things New Age. A day in Venice Beach reveals tarot card readers along the esplanade, on the other side of which lies trendy shops, among them a number of New Age stores that sell everything from crystals to spell candles, and alkalised water charged with sound frequencies.

At one such store, the Aura Shop, the people running it acknowledge that some of their customers don't quite get how it all works. They tell people, 'We're not here to fix you.' They don't want co-dependents. They offer tools.

'We've still got to snap people out of it,' the owner tells me. 'Every day they walk in here and they have no idea that it's actually mostly them that's going to make this [pointing at a crystal] or anything else effective.'

Back to Stacey, she has personally found resonance in the myth of Artemis — she who is wild and free, a huntress who dwells in the forest. In a legend, Artemis saves a friend of her father, the god Zeus. To reward his daughter, Zeus declares he will find a husband for her. Artemis isn't interested, though. She tells Zeus that a better reward would be to let her run free in the forest — that she can be independent and her own woman. Marriage is her choice, and if she wants to be alone, please leave her to it.

'I read that story as a young woman and went, *That's what I want. There's a role model there for me.* I didn't have to be like everybody else.'

I am curious, though, about how this belief works in Stacey's mind. 'I believe that the world, and the universe, and the creative power of that is the expression of a creative force.'

But does she believe Artemis literally existed, or is it an energy humans call Artemis that represents a certain aspect of us? Particularly given there are god and goddess equivalents across cultures. Does it even matter at all?

'My definition here would be: it doesn't matter. I have had enough experiences, weird or not, that have given me the idea that there is an energy . . . and whether or not I've cultivated it, whether it's part of my consciousness and behaviour, whether it's separate, it doesn't really matter to me. But she has influenced how I've grown up, how I've seen myself. I believe we are attracted to the goddesses we most need. And, for me, I needed a strong female role model to show me what to do.' The important point, Stacey says, is to praise and learn from these deities.

And let's talk about mythos. You'll find Western authors are retelling myths of ancient deities — Neil Gaiman with *Norse Mythology*, Madeleine Miller with *Circe*, Colm Tóibín with *House of Names* and Stephen Fry with *Mythos*. They remain popular because they are instructive: narratives where gods and goddesses, despite being immortal, behave just like humans, and teach us about what it means to be one through story.

'Mythos is a language,' says Stacey, who doesn't use the term 'myth'. She makes this distinction because, for the Greeks, *mythos* went hand in hand with *logos*: myth and logic. Back then, 'Myth meant a story with a truth. It didn't mean a lie, like it does now.' She points to the Bible, Norse mythology, ancient Arabia — stories that held within them a core truth, from which lessons can be learned.

I confide to Stacey that I'm finding a lot in these stories of old. The way I have experienced life as a woman from a culture that has particular ideas about how women should behave and exist in the world. I'm trying some things out. Reinvesting in creative passions I once had but left by the wayside. Improv theatre lessons once a week, for starters. Acting lessons, too.

Stacey looks ready to burst with excitement. She's known me for a while, I suppose; gets that this is important for me, that I'm on a path, seeking — perhaps not communion with mythological deities, but with myself. That I am enjoying rituals on occasion, quietly in search of new ways of thinking and being in the world. Willing to be led the best way, because I needlessly complicate my routes and usually get disoriented anyway.

Stacey is careful about appearing a spokesperson for witches. She emphasises that the way of modern paganism, which allows you to pull from lots of different traditions, is not every witch's way. 'It's such a different path. Like we don't have a pagan pope, we don't have a clergy. The majority of witches — and this is what people need to really get — are solitary and they're eclectic.'

Stacey is speaking of her pagan path; she is not Wiccan, which she says is a tradition, not a belief system. 'You can be a witch and not Wiccan, but if you're a Wiccan, you're a witch.'

Witchcraft really can't be simplified to even just a couple of approaches; you can be Wiccan or a pagan witch, but the kind of witch you are is shaped by magic and ritual. For example, Thelema witchcraft was founded by Aleister Crowley and draws on ancient Egyptian rituals. Some traditions are region-based — Celtic and Druid witches focus on Celtic magic, European witches follow European magic. There are elemental witches (working with air, fire, water, earth and spirit), and ceremonial witches (who use ceremony and ritual in their craft).

But while there is freedom in being a witch, like all traditions, there are also boundaries. A key moral tenet for witches is to do what you will, but harm none.

As for sceptics or those critical of her polytheistic beliefs, Stacey says she's come to expect the hate mail that reaches her once or twice a week on Facebook or in the mail, from people who want to kill her, save her or believe she's going to hell. She doesn't respond to strangers on Facebook Messenger.

'If I'm going to get hated on, it's more for the fact that I support the Sea Shepherd, or [that] I'm quite active in the environmental area. After all, I'm earth honouring.' Stacey's tenor changes when she talks about human destruction of the environment. 'When somebody does that, it's like pissing in my temple.'

When we're about to wrap up, Stacey tells me that Natureluster, her program to help people connect to nature, will always be free. 'The most spiritual thing I do is that. Keeping people connected with nature.'

She sees it as more than grounding. 'We have global warming happening. If everyone was more connected with nature and what is happening right now, do you think that we would have the problems that we're having now?'

As we're leaving, Stacey reminds me of Artemis and her story. 'Go out in nature. Walk through a park, through nature. She's a moving god. Everyone comes to her when they're ready. If she had come ten years earlier, I wouldn't have been ready.'

Anatomy of a spell

Stacey wants to demystify and simplify witchcraft and magic. In practical terms, she says spellcraft is actually an everyday occurrence. Have you ever made a wish on a dandelion, or when you blew out the candles on your birthday cake?

'There are plenty of little spells we do in real life that we don't really think of as spells,' she says, adding that everybody has the ability to do this.

You can hold off on buying cauldrons and the like though. You don't need equipment. Stacey actually bans her students from using any for the first three months. But there are tools that witches use, including wands and potions, which she says are meant to focus your energy. 'I've got different wands. I really loathe to tell people about wands in the beginning because everyone wants one and they don't even know how to use it. Wands are simply something that channel energy. They don't have energy of their own.'

Witches also use herbs, which are an ancient ingredient in magic, as are a more recent favourite, crystals. Witches might make up potions, or poppet and herbal bags as tools for ritual.

A basic candle will do for beginners, based on the following example. Spellcraft, Stacey says, is a rational practice that can be applied to anything, and it involves five points: purpose and intention, focus, raising power, release and participation.

1. Decide what you want (purpose and intention).
2. Concentrate while lighting a candle (focus).
3. Tap into your emotion, your yearning (raising power).
4. Send it out by blowing out the candle (release).
5. Be alert to signs and situations that will help you take action towards your goal (participation).

In spellcraft, a core rule is: Don't interfere with another person's free will. If, for example, someone wants to attract a partner, Stacey will never cast a spell on a particular love interest; instead, she will help someone cast on themselves so that they can better find a suitable partner.

And looking for love is only one of the most common themes. 'Nothing has changed in thousands of years,' Stacey says. 'Everybody wants more money, to be happy in love, and then within that, things like conceiving a child . . . And the other thing is health. People want to lose weight.'

And if you're wondering how a spell to lose weight would actually work, the idea is not that you wake up lighter the next morning. If your desire is to lose weight, you may find yourself led to a suitable way to do that.

Any spell is designed to channel your intention, so that higher divine forces can lead you to a solution or dissolve barriers to one. You are the key participant in your evolution. The ritual of it is a way to focus your energy, contain it with intention and be still enough that your mind does not get in the way. This is why so many different things work — you need to find the thing that makes this possible for you.

Witchcraft has a complex image. While I am not a witch myself, the ones I know never fail to get me thinking about how I connect to the world around me, and to myself. I have, obviously, learned a great deal from Stacey; she has succeeded in opening people up to the potential of magic and witchcraft, whether or not they choose to follow it as a life path.

In recent times, we have seen the continued scrutiny of harmful practices of magic in media headlines. One celebrity famously sacrifices chickens in ritual. There are other worrying stories about the occult, but for my part, and this is perhaps because I grew up being judged for my religious and cultural heritage, I believe that witchcraft is not the issue, just some people's practice of it. Witchcraft can mean positive change, or, as Stacey suggests, being a catalyst for transformation.

RITUAL MAGIC AND THE OCCULT

Glastonbury, in the English county of Somerset, is a place of woo woo. A goddess temple sits unobtrusively among shops that offer all things New Age, from readings to books and clothing. It attracts visitors to the Chalice Well, also known as the 'Red Spring', the name given to the natural spring because of its reddish hue due to iron oxide deposits. It's said to have healing qualities. People do rituals there, bottle up the water and take it home with them.

Glastonbury attracts tourists for both the well and Glastonbury Tor, a famous hill that, at its top, has a monument — the ruins of St Michael's Tower. It's a steep climb to reach the top. I'm one of several visitors, but who knows what brings us all here? There are those who come for the mysticism of the land, or a love of mythology; others out of curiosity or because they've been dragged there by a family member who is a believer.

The Tor is an impressive sight. But as I climb to its peak, I feel little else but unsettled, and I don't know why. At the top, I push aside my unease and wander around, then sit for a while and contemplate life as a harsh wind beats against my face. Then I rise from my spot and slowly make my way down. All of a sudden, I trip and fall hard. So hard that my jeans rip and my knees are left a bloodied mess.

I don't embrace paranormal experiences. For all of my fascination with the supernatural, I have no interest in conjuring spirits or seeing ghosts. But it feels uncannily like I was shoved down the hill.

Friends who are woo woo-literate offered varying explanations ('You weren't welcome'; 'Archangel Michael was giving you a metaphorical push that he took too literally'; 'If I had known you were going there, I would've told you to stay away . . .'). But as I sit down to discuss all things otherworldly with my friend Christian Read, I realise that he's probably the most equipped to offer an interesting insight on what happened at the Tor. He's seen and done things as a practising ritual magician, and as a horror writer who specialises in the occult and ceremonial magic. His partner, Michelle, who is also with us, also knows a thing or two about mystical creatures and experiences.

Sure enough, Christian doesn't blink. 'Definitely faeries.'

I take this the same way I did my friend's Archangel Michael declaration: with a pound of salt. I suppose I believe in some version of faeries but I see them less as Tinkerbell types with wings and more as spirits inhabiting the earth and working with its elements.

The Tor is the realm of King Arthur, supposedly where he was taken after he died. Christian adds more to the story: 'It came out of an earlier tradition of Celtic mythology, and it's where Malagant, who was the half-faery warlord, used to live in his castle of glass.'

Christian looks a bit amused. 'I'd be very surprised if the infamously racist white tradition of King Arthur was particularly fond of . . .'

'An Arab woman on their territory?'

We have a laugh.

'Well, Morien, one of King Arthur's knights, was a Moor, so you never know. Maybe it was him. He was jealous, you cutting in on his action.'

Michelle chimes in, 'Also, if it was faeries, they might've just thought it was funny.'

It's never dull speaking to Christian and Michelle. I am friends with both of them, having become acquainted when I worked with Michelle as a sub-editor in my early days of journalism. Nowadays, she is an acclaimed science writer, but she also knows faeries.

'What, they thought it would be hilarious to get me?'

'Yeah. Faeries don't operate on the same morality levels as humans,' she says, matter-of-fact.

Well, all right then. I am already drawn into this intriguing realm. 'If we're going to speak about faeries, let's say what they are perhaps? If they exist, they are energies, right? Like jinn?'

'I mean there's a whole tradition of what faeries are,' says Christian.

'Do you believe in them?'

'I believe that humans have the ability to have contact with things that can feel non-human. And it doesn't matter if they're real or not; what counts is the feeling.'

That feeling is something humans have sought for millenia, through prayer and ritual. Magic is a specific way of encountering something that is perhaps outside yourself, but definitely within yourself, Christian explains. I can't argue with this. 'You have that experience. You felt that experience. You felt that contact with something that isn't human. Maybe it's something within yourself. Maybe it's something outside yourself. It doesn't matter. You still had that experience.'

Anthropologists call it a non-ordinary reality. It's the shamanic state, ecstasy, a poetic state. It's what Christian's magical mob calls *gnosis* (knowledge).

'You put yourself in a very elevated consciousness, which anyone has experienced. A football player experiences it, an actor experiences it performing on stage. Athletes call it The Zone. Religious people might call it ecstasy. Anyone can enter into a non-ordinary reality at any time.'

The goal of magic — ritual or ceremonial — practised as it is today is to enter into that space, and to experience something. 'Maybe to experience something, and acquire knowledge to assist in your life.'

There is nothing outrageously woo woo about Christian. You wouldn't pick that he practises ritual magic in the privacy of his home if you encountered him in a café. He is all for the flair and ritual in the context of ceremonial magic — a cape, a robe, props like a wand, objects that symbolise the elements. But outside of this, he is dressed like anybody else. He is also a grounded guy. Casual, easy and interesting to talk to, with a sharpness and a wit that will slice through any inauthenticity. He does have a fair few interesting tattoos that speak to his lifestyle and, strikingly to me, he wears a cross. Not because he worships Jesus — he's not into religion. 'I irreligiously admire the life of Christ as a social reformer and spiritual figure; I do not religiously worship him.'

'If you want to argue, for the sake of my research, that the point of self-help or spirituality is to evolve as a person, what is the point of magic?' I ask. 'Does magic help you to evolve or transform, or is the point just the giddiness of an experience that dissipates? Or does it stay with you?'

'The heart of magic, the great work — and this is what they call it — is literally about transformation,' says Christian.

In ritual magic, Christian uses evocation, where he tries to summon the spirit of the god and talk to the god. 'This is a very common pagan practice,' he says. 'Wiccans are keen on *invocation* — commonly thought of as a prayer, but in magic it's actually where a person pretends to be the god by channelling the energy of that deity through them.

'I don't have anybody to do that with, and I'm not that comfortable with it anyway,' continues Christian. 'But an *evocation* is where you're trying to get the god to talk directly to you. For me it mainly happens in spectacularly vivid dreams. And I always know [when the dream is an evocation] . . . it feels quantitatively different to me, the experience of the dream; it feels clearer. It feels more concrete. It feels like I'm much less conscious of having a dream. And I feel like I'm actually in the scenario depicted and, generally speaking, I will be given demonstrations of what to do.'

In ritual practice, he is not always specific. 'Sometimes you just go, OK, who's got a message for me? Who's out there? Who wants to talk? Whatever creatures are out there, please manifest yourself.' He goes into his dedicated space with a notepad and pen, and an offering, something that involves sacrifice of some kind. A glass of whisky that he throws out, rather than drinks; some money that he later gives away as his payment to the entities working with him. The wisdom, he says, isn't necessarily free.

'In ritual practice, you have to be working yourself up into an elevated state of consciousness. There are various ways you can do that.'

Add anything to create a mood and setting: candles, incense, music. The aim is to change your state. 'And it's literally just the tools of acting. Props, clothes, hair, make-up . . . And then you will enter into a state where you want to change your consciousness. Now you could do that through drugs. You could do that through — not to be rude — sex and pleasure. You could do that through exhaustion.' Christian cites dervishes, spinning themselves into this elevated state. The well-practised Christian simply meditates. 'I might read out some prayers to myself.'

Christian is particularly fond of a book called *The Book of Abramelin*, which relates to sacred magic. He can read grimoires of the works of authors he admires, then use something as simple as breath control to change his state. And he follows his own written instructions — it is ritual magic, after all. 'There might be a prayer, there might be an incantation, literally a spell, instructions to myself: feel this, do this, point in that direction and make this gesture. And generally speaking, by that point in time, you either know if you've got it or you don't.' Not every process is a success, because the magician is seeking a verifiable experience that records what was felt and whether or not it worked.

'If I experienced what you might call the divine, that would be meeting a god figure. But to me, it's the interfacing with the information of the god. If I needed a strategy . . . I might dedicate something to Mars, the god of war, because he wasn't just the god of fighting, he was the god of strategies. If I wanted money, I might go to Plutus, the god of money.'

I already know the answer, knowing Christian, but I ask anyway. 'Have you done that?'

'Uh, no, but I could.' Christian is averse to misuse of magic, say, to gain wealth. 'I'm not very interested in how magic affects my material life. I'm interested in what it teaches me about myself and what it teaches me about other people.'

This taps into what I see as the New Age's greatest challenge — the process of guiding people towards less suffering and more peace, emphasising an inward journey, rather than material riches. You could argue, as many a self-help and spiritual leader have, that you change your internal world and the exterior one around you reflects this.

Christian has multiple sclerosis, a chronic condition that sees him in pain much of the day. In ritual, he spoke to the demigod of healing, Asclepius, to Thoth, the Egyptian god of wisdom and knowledge, and Dian Cecht, the Celtic god of medicine. 'It helped me put things in perspective and it gave me strategies for coping.'

'Could you give me an example of something where you've received a solution or guidance for your pain, for example?'

'Yes, actually,' he says, brightly. 'Medical marijuana.'

A few weeks earlier, Christian was featured in a story on medical marijuana usage on the ABC website in Australia, in which he speaks of the benefits of the treatment.

His explanation is an example of how magical requests work: a request to find a solution or treatment to help, made with deities, which resulted in a dream where the god Thoth guided Christian to medical marijuana. 'I asked my neurologist because I had to see her a few days later and she said, "Ha, you're in luck. One of the very, very few people who currently prescribes medical marijuana is at the local GP centre." So it worked out perfectly for me.'

Christian works almost entirely alone, in a regular practice — a minimum of once a month, but more commonly, it's a weekly appointment. He doesn't talk shop with magician friends. 'I find that an online community is useful to have.'

There are communities, groups and even secret societies, of course. Many people work in ritual groups, Christian says, citing the Rosicrucian Order (Ancient Mystical Order Rosae Crucis, or the AMORC) as probably the biggest organised ritual magical group. 'And they're ultimately akin to a religion; they're much more religious in nature. They have services, they have a mass, and they are very much based on Western occultism.'

'Anyone can go and join the Gnostic church or the Order of the Golden Dawn or even your local Satanist group if you like. They're very cool at the moment.'

'I'm right, thanks.' It's an automatic response. I may be a seeker, but I don't need to see all the sights.

While Christian is open to traditions, he avoids dabbling in culturally specific ones like voodoo. 'But I feel very connected to Graeco-Roman tradition. I feel very connected to the Kabbalah.' Kabbalah is an ancient mystical arm of Judaism, which became popular among celebrities in the early 2000s.

Magic can be a very intellectually rigorous tradition; the expectation to read old books is partly what separates magicians from the more generalised New Age, says Christian.

But what if you still want to do magic but not the homework?

Chaos magic.

Christian is in alignment with the chaos magic movement born in the 1970s. Chaos is generally spoken of as some dark underbelly of magic. Raw, boundless, and absent of the uplifting sheen of New Age-type endeavours. People who are magic-literate might steer you towards or away from it. But Christian says chaos magic is just magic that you invent, or magic that has been invented for you. It's about hands-on experimentation.

The Encyclopedia of Magic & Witchcraft says chaos differs from other magical practices in that it 'is not a spiritual path', nor does it rely on strict ritual or belief. It has been influenced by nineteenth-century occultists Aleister Crowley and Austin Osman Spare, as well as the works of

Peter J. Carroll, whose books *Liber Null* and *Psychonaut* are considered important texts in chaos magic. The maxim 'Nothing is true, everything is permitted' can be found in Carroll's *Principia Chaotica*.

'In the 1970s, people were looking to throw off old traditions,' Christian says. 'Things were moving forward culturally.' What else was happening at the tail end of the 1970s? Punk. 'There was an attempt to break away with the traditions of elders . . . All the tensions revolving around World War II had well and truly worn out.'

Christian encourages people to try any kind of ritual work. 'I think it's interesting. I think it's psychologically rewarding. And I think it's curious and fun.'

He isn't concerned about people attempting magic through commercialised offerings, like a witchcraft kit at Sephora.

I have to call him on this. For someone who has a passion for ceremonial magic, surely buying a kit in a chain store moves him in some way?

'I think it's good. I think you should try it. And I think that if you need to get started by buying a kit, go nuts.'

The notion of authenticity in occultism is not useful, he says. It's not about what's real, but the experience of it. I take Christian's point. It goes to the core of my journey: the experiences of spiritual practice, rather than the appearance of them.

Besides, magic is not culturally specific. It passes through cultures quickly and efficiently. This is called 'syncretism'. 'This is why you might get a Catholic folk saint [in evocation]. That's ultimately a spiritual figure with its basis in Aztec mythology,' Christian says.

I am not a ritual magician, but I suspect some of my

personal rituals, which to me have spiritual provenance, could be classified as chaos magic under Christian's broad definition. Consider the ways you set out to achieve goals, unclutter a confused mind, find new directions and so on. When I need to complete a task and I'm struggling, I might light a candle and ask for help. I have created mandala drawings to centre myself when I'm adrift and seeking clarity. I have written down wishes and desires as though they are already with me, quietly rising into that elevated state as I did so. I have attended workshops where we have danced or engaged in ritual without religious or any kind of deity reference.

For me, what all of these have in common is that power of 'experience' Christian describes; moments of connection and insight, or a feeling of trust that answers will come. It is about being in a moment of communion — with other people or an invisible realm. It can be a cleansing or uplifting surrender.

It does not have to be complicated or grandiose. It does not have to be your way of life. But I think, if you're so inclined to include ritual in your life, respect your processes — or those of others if you're not working solo — and simply own it. It does not have to feel magical, but perhaps you can allow for magic to happen, whatever that looks like for you.

MANIFESTATION, FATE & DESTINY

At one stage of gainful full-time employment, I would often begin my day in a local food court. It was a quiet time of the morning, when I had space to sit and think, to formulate my ideas about what I wanted from life.

I had reached a stage where I didn't quite know where I was headed, but I knew I was on my way. Despite my impatient energy, I can be a slow mover, at the mercy of external factors. No matter how much we want something, it may not be forthcoming, or if it's available to us, it may not be the right time.

About a decade ago, I found my feet as a journalist, with a specialty in writing and editing features in trade publications. By the time I was working in the property industry, my growth was more assured. I had come to include regular physical activity, meditations and affirmations into my daily routine. The results were evident to me, though I didn't try to quantify them in any particular way. I was healthier, more content, and life was bursting with opportunities I had never imagined possible. I was writing more creatively. I had self-published my first book, finally moving on from the disappointment of a publishing deal falling through.

And in the food court those mornings, I would scrawl desires and possibilities without thinking. Some might call this automatic writing, but I wasn't channelling messages. I was writing down, without censoring myself, the way I envisioned life could be. I'm not quite sure what led me to do that so effortlessly. Perhaps it was a release, or a way to feel into my desires and what seemed realistic.

Months after I began, I was chatting with a work colleague. I don't remember how we came to the subject of manifestation, but she said she swore by a certain technique. She would write things down, she told me, as though they had already happened. And it would work.

I realised I was doing something similar. Not channelling external wisdom, but plumbing my own depths for knowledge of myself. Life seemed more open to possibility; I was 'adulting' later than I had hoped, but I was doing it nonetheless. I filled tiny notebooks, but I never looked at them again. I'm not sure I'd be able to read them all — my notoriously bad handwriting was unintelligible by the end of a session.

Years later, though, when I was moving into my first home with my husband, Chris, I found one of the notebooks. I smiled as I flipped through it, feeling some affection for the young woman who sat parcelling her dreams into notebooks before work.

I stopped at a particular page, where my hopes for a nice partner exploded on the page. I don't remember much, but one line stayed with me; 'He is already here,' I had written. I flipped through the notebook and found this exact expression more than once.

I think those words slid through me at the time. I assumed whoever he was would be someone in my 'circle'. Around me, not too far, and I may not even know him yet.

But when I wrote it, my now-husband Chris was in my life as my manager at work. We were also friends who enjoyed each other's company, and I learned so much from him about writing, journalism and life in general. But the relationship was always professional.

I had never imagined Chris as my future husband. I admired him, thought of him as a decent man, and I knew he would be a good partner. But I wasn't asking for him specifically. Maybe just someone like him.

Obviously, if I had written: 'He is already here (it's Chris!!!!)', I wouldn't have paid much attention because the idea would have seemed ludicrous. We were colleagues, Chris was in a relationship, and he was very much not a Muslim.

And yet . . .

Obviously, I did not 'manifest' him, but the exercise did something. It helped me to engineer my wishes to an extent, to think differently about the possibilities of my life, and to be open to new doorways. It helped to clarify my desires and goals, and to orient myself purposefully towards them. Not everything would be up to me; good fortune helps, but that, I find, tends to appear when you make an effort.

At other times, I have desired certain things and energetically 'put it out there', and when those desires were fulfilled, I've wondered if it was in response to my call, or just a matter of me signing the delivery slip on an order that was already on its way.

When I write, sometimes things I have imagined come true, either literally or in essence. Elizabeth Gilbert's book *Big Magic* is all about this world of 'transcendent' ideas. In the book, Gilbert makes clear her perspectives on the spiritual and magical undertones of creative experience. She unequivocally expresses belief in magic and her devotion to living in a world of enchantment.

I see elements of this in my own work. Sometimes, when I view a film or read a book that transports me,

I reflect on the creative method; I acknowledge the dedication and craft. What are we tapping into when we write? How did this idea find me? And how does it connect to the way I have lived and what I've been through? There is an alchemy to it.

I have examples that to this day leave me in awe. Things I have written for characters that would form part of my own journey rather than simply reflect it.

When I was writing a draft of a novel about an Arab woman who has lost her identity and will make peace with it in the homeland, I had her in the desert outskirts of Jordan in the Arab world. During this time, following a massage, my therapist commented: 'I'm not sure what you're writing, but you're in the desert kicking up sand.' And months later, I was the Arab woman in the desert kicking up sand, having moved on from the novel to a non-fiction exploration of the lives of Arab women.

My fictional character had visited Zaatari refugee camp as a journalist before travelling on to Palestine, with a sick father at home. Months later, that was me, recording interviews for ABC Radio National and my book. That was me, a woman making peace with her blurred identity, a father fresh out of hospital back home.

I marvelled at this; I had partially lived out what I'd written. Not the whole story, obviously. My character was not me, even if I understood what it was to be her. But I don't believe I manifested those events. Perhaps, I think even now, I was simply drawing on what was to come.

Manifestation is perhaps the New Age's greatest selling point, the big name on the woo woo marquee. Thoughts-creating-reality is a popular belief of the think-it-or-write-it-and-it-is-done school of thought. Then there are other less cerebral approaches to manifestation: casting a spell, drawing a mandala, creating a vision board, or setting up a crystal grid. Or even, let's say, when you assign meaning to an object so that it becomes a talisman. All of these require a level of surrender; a slipping into a different state of consciousness in order to get out of your own way and make room for divine assistance. Similarly, meditations can be thought of in this way.

Dr Joe Dispenza is one of the increasing number of New Age writers who delve into the quantum field, that invisible plane of infinite possibilities that connects all beings and things. Dispenza explains in his bestselling book, *Breaking the Habit of Being Yourself*, that it is a passion of his to 'demystify the mystical' so that people can experience personal transformation, having mystical experiences that transcend language.

Dispenza doesn't have the audience of, say, Tony Robbins, but his books are available far and wide. He's a New Age phenomenon. He has a level of charisma, but if Robbins is the rock star of self-help and empowerment, Dispenza is like the slightly dorky but reputable soccer dad everyone likes.

During a quiet time, having just written a non-fiction book and on the lookout for next steps, I had dinner with a friend. We got talking about how woo woo we can be, and she told me how much she loves Dispenza. I downloaded some of his meditations. While you really need to start with his books to get a handle on what he's leading you through and towards — he wants you to become a 'supernatural genius' — I have to say, doing some of his meditations seemed to break through the heavy silence of my world at the time. I didn't 'manifest' so much as 'reveal'. Suddenly, my vista expanded. I went from feeling limited in my aspirations, to remembering dreams long held but abandoned or forgotten.

'You are the creator of your own life,' he tells us at a day seminar in Melbourne, 'Becoming Supernatural', a few months after I first listened to his meditations. He says the same sort of thing in a more condensed version at CYL in Phoenix.

Dispenza smiles a lot, like he's wondering why not everyone gets it, that you can be the creator of your own life. He offers up a variation on a famous expression, quoted most notably by Anaïs Nin: 'You don't see things how they are. You see things how you are.'

He urges people to invest in changing their energy daily, to change their world. Dispenza's purpose is rooted in addressing detrimental habits and healing the sick.

I want to believe this. He presents slide after slide of research showing how the brain changes in meditation. His book *You Are The Placebo* is jam-packed with case studies. I have a friend who attended one of his advanced retreats and attests to spontaneous healings. This sort of thing makes me wince. I don't discount the possibility at all that a mental state can affect your physical one. This is not to say how you think causes illness, but people do get sick due to stress and trauma. How a person feels mentally can arguably affect how they heal or experience an illness or a condition. But miraculous, spontaneous healing? I'm dubious about it. I think a lot of what Dispenza has to say can be very helpful to people struggling to let go of the past and release regrets. Not that I'll be signing up to his retreats in exotic places. As insightful as I find his work, I have no interest in becoming devoted to a particular person or their teachings. It can spiral out of control (and cost you a bomb); you can wind up getting lost in the practice, not stopping long enough to see if it's actually working.

While Dispenza wants to provide a working model for manifesting your best life, and he taps into the divine, more frequently people like Dispenza are eschewing this kind of terminology for more scientific language. Atoms and particles and the like. In magical work, it's about changing your mental state to one beyond thought.

Oprah Winfrey, who is all about creating your best life, even talked about manifestation when promoting her film, *A Wrinkle in Time*. The interviewer for BlackTree TV, Jaleesa Lashay, confessed that interviewing Oprah was on her vision board for 2018, 'and I'm here, so I have manifested this moment'. Oprah rushed to give her a hug while singing out gloriously, Oprah-style.

Lashay asked Oprah where she sits with vision boards. Oprah explained that she has dispensed with them — she's 'a powerful manifestor' and she can achieve results without the physical action of the board. She went on to describe what is commonly believed about how you can manifest: connecting to the 'vibration' of the thing or experience. You need to feel into it, and not be held back by your fears of not getting what you want. You need to tap into the feeling of what it will look like if you do get it. This alignment also means you need to be ready to accept this desire when it unfolds in your life.

When I attended conscious dance in Los Angeles following the CYL conference, the instructor, Jo Cobbett, and I got to talking about manifestation and she said something similar. 'The emotional commitment in the meditation, to the practice, is what makes it successful, and most of the other vehicles for meditation don't involve that kind of emotion,' she says. 'I'm putting the mind into a meditative state, but I'm heightening my emotional field so I'm creating this' — Jo makes a whoosh sound — 'moment like.'

I know what she's talking about. It's built-up energy that meets a thought of your desire or intention. Dispenza calls this moment the 'elevated emotion'. In his book *Becoming Supernatural*, he shows you how to 'tune in' to new possibilities in the quantum field. This involves drawing up your desires and assigning a letter. The elevated emotions arise when you think about how having your desire will feel. I saw similarities to a method of chaos magic that uses sigils, which are symbols used in ritual. In chaos, the magician renders an abstract sigil to reflect the outcome they seek.

I wonder, though: is all manifestation an attempt at directing the 'universe', of imposing your will on it? Or is it just a wish, a prayer, a hope sent out into the ether? *Or* is it you tuning in to what already exists? Like you're watering flowers you didn't know existed in the garden of your life?

Like many people, I was brought up on a staple of belief regarding fate. Arabs, and Muslims in particular, talk about *naseeb*. This is your fate, where things like your relationships (marriage), life path (purpose/place in the world) and your end (you don't have a say in this) are already in your life's blueprint. A friend told me your forehead has an invisible imprint of the name of your spouse (which led me to make jokes about Elizabeth Taylor because she had several husbands and her forehead would have gotten quite crowded). When someone dies, it's their *naseeb* to have died then and in that way. When something doesn't work out for you, despite your most ardent desires, *ma fish naseeb* (it wasn't destined to be).

Arguably this can work in your favour if you're having a hard time convincing your parents of something. While my parents are highly protective and loving, and I know have only ever wanted the best for me, 'the best' is based on their sensibilities and world views. So when I have brought home men they weren't sold on, they've resisted but would also reflect, 'If that's her *naseeb* . . .'

I have a more gentle engagement with all of this nowadays. Like I'm moving towards possibility but also pathways that seem to link to my desires. Perhaps I didn't choose writing, it chose me for what I would bring to it that is different from others.

One day, as I was saying goodbye to my parents after an outing, I remember talking to my mother about my life choices in career. I am a law graduate, and I practised briefly before admitting to myself that it was not my desired path. I know my parents were disappointed, and perhaps still wonder about what seemed to them like a foolish decision. Sometimes, on a particularly difficult day in a profession that is notoriously challenging for those wishing to make a living out of it, I wonder, too: what if I had chosen that challenging but ultimately more stable path of being a lawyer?

I was about to head to my car when my mother grew quite still and said, 'You were given the hands to write and the mouth to speak.' There was something to how she said it: like it was a declaration sent through her for me to understand. The way she punched her fist into the air as she said it, the way she looked me in the eye.

My mother is a private person. She worries about me being in the public eye. But to her, this is my path. This is my *naseeb*.

Some things have always been questionable to me in this area, though. Does our inherent nature dictate how we live in this world to an extent? And can we overcome our darkest parts? The parts that may cause harm to others, knowingly or without intention? If things are predetermined, why are we judged from a religious perspective? The answers were always vague, mainly because they are hard to prove or quantify — personal experiences don't necessarily cut it. Most people I knew would tell me that I do have choice, that God just knows what I am going to do.

Perhaps it's more clearly explained in the way various religions and traditions look at it: free will and predetermination co-exist. We don't have as much control as we think we do, or would like to; consider all of the environmental and human issues with which we must deal on a daily basis. And yet, daily, we make choices, big and small.

The psychics (also called 'intuitives') I have spoken to talk about providing options and pathways in life, about not offering definitive guidance to the person having a reading (called 'querents' in the divination world). I realise this may be difficult to accept for some, but there are genuinely good people working in the New Age world with the hope of improving the lives of others. They feel the responsibility of giving insight. They wrestle with how to assist someone who just wants a quick and hopeful answer to, 'When will he come back?'

In that piece I wrote about divination for *SBS Life*, Lindel Barker-Revell, a clairvoyant, astrologer, tea-leaf reader and founder of Tea-wise, told me: 'When people come for a reading, they do want to know about the future, but they also should be given free will within that, because we're all offered many options every day; in tiny little ways, we make choices.'

In that same article, energy intuitive Denise Jarvie offered: 'Divination of old implies that you have no choice, that things will just arrive in your life and this is your lot. We are left pondering what we did wrong or right to have this thing arrive in our life.'

And self-described 'insight facilitator' Kerstin Fehn offered this: 'The common idea that I can see the future as a set path of events, like houses in a street, and can therefore tell you what's happening step by step, is really tough to deal with. The reality, for me, is that the future depends on decisions, and the influences on those decisions produce more like a city of streets or a tapestry. Some avenues are closer, some are being built. Some have stop signs. And if you haven't made a decision, there is open sea. Therefore, readings are better used to check in with yourself: am I making the right decisions? What's the quickest path? The most fun?'

I think there is truth to the idea that we can have a say in how our lives unfold, but only to an extent, given how much is beyond our control. You can ask for something, but it could take a while for it to show up (and what have you done in that time to help it along its way?). Possibilities and opportunities can be brought into view in a meditative or intuitive state, but perhaps they already exist and are waiting for us. So are we simply coming into alignment with what is already there? Take the example of the weight loss spell Stacey Demarco mentioned earlier in the chapter. The weight loss spell is a request for assistance in getting your body back into balance. You've sent out a beacon and, through ritual, changed your state to one that is more receptive. Perhaps, yes, invisible forces are at work, but you needed to show up, too.

In all of this, my concern lies in the idea of asking for stuff that (a) doesn't really belong to you, and (b) would be a really bad idea if it did. So you can draw up some plans, or make a request, but what are you really asking for?

Also, it's worth noting that many New Age participants and teachers are focused on service to humanity and the earth. A commonly used phrase is 'for the greater good', often included in invocations for healing of any kind. A gentle reminder that we're all in this together, even if we don't always act like it.

If you take anything away from this, it's that manifestation techniques all mirror some essential elements:

intention, raised energy, surrender to synchronicity and divine timing.

They all require that 'moment', where your emotion is beyond ordinary consciousness, where you're feeling the result of your desire as though it's already in existence. Most instructors on this will remind you that divine timing is at play in our lives. Like Miracle Max says in *The Princess Bride*, 'Don't rush me, sonny. You rush a miracle man, you get rotten miracles.'

I have mixed feelings about all of this. I have trouble with the idea that we can 'manifest' something. Rather, I think we're just tuning in, calling in something we sense as a desire within ourselves. In her deck *Sacred Rebels Oracle*, Alana Fairchild has a card that says 'What you want, wants you'. It's reassurance that what you desire is hurtling its way towards you, but you must make effort towards receiving it. When Joseph Campbell says to 'follow your bliss', he is suggesting the same idea: pay attention to those niggling feelings, those nudges, the things you feel effortlessly passionate about.

In the US, Tamara Dunne, a transitional life coach I met with for my research, also offers this as a possibility. I tell her about my recent explorations of interests I have always felt drawn to but never thought possible for me: 'Something that you fantasised about when you were younger — was it a fantasy or was it your intuition?'

Jasmine Hawkins, a healer who does what could be described as 'psychic surgery' — clearing blocks, untying cosmically-made knots and cutting cords — also questions this. 'Of course I do believe we can draw things to ourselves. I also think if the soul has something in store already planned, that a person can get a sense that it is coming. And then when it actually does come, they say, "Oh, look, I manifested it".'

For example, a trip to Italy you dreamed about then manifested? It was always meant to happen; you found yourself wanting something that wanted you back. 'I think it's seeded.'

Then there's another interesting take to consider from self-help author and psychologist Gay Hendricks, whose work certainly has a spiritual thread. In his book *The Joy of Genius*, he suggests that the more you engage with your genius, the more good luck chases you because it 'chases the expression of genius'. In this case, he is talking about capitalising on your innate, natural abilities to truly find flow.

Others will identify this as simply being in creative flow, of being on your path, where there is no need to exert effort or force things. This should feel good. Life may not always be easy, but you're not so easily stuck, lost or worried about what you're missing out on.

To me, this idea sounds like it's drawn from the Vedic tradition, which advises to 'follow charm'. Angela Lyos Braun, my Vedic meditation teacher, refers to 'a fine level of feeling' that leads you on a road to evolution.

I suppose, if you really wanted to manifest something out of a pure desire, you could give it a try. Maybe it will even work. But then, I'm not sure who you're speaking to, or what deal you're making with the invisible world, in order to get that. Much like the realm of magic, manifestation should not be abused for personal gain. Magic is really about that search for experience and truth. Manifestation can get lost with its indulgent, potentially egotistical approach to material gain. I would dare say that your life will be better with a focus on manifesting a more peaceful and balanced life, where fulfilment can come though the inner and outer worlds, but isn't reliant on material possessions.

As always, be careful what you wish for and who or what might be affected if you get it. You see examples of people having things they seem at odds with — a partner in the marriage they longed for; the car they fantasised about; the job they thought would make them feel whole. I have heard many stories of manifestations that were successful, but not what the person thought it would be. My favourite was a woman telling me she did a spell for a very specific love interest to enter her life. A few days later, a man fitting the description appeared in her life. They went out on a date but there was no chemistry, even though he ticked the boxes.

In any case, you've heard the saying, 'Just put it out there.' That's your call-out, a request sent out into the unknown. But I would argue that this is usually (and preferably) the result of some inner knowing. You have tuned in to your desires, and those desires are reflecting what is already coming into form.

PRACTICAL MAGIC

Regardless of what you believe, if you work with manifestation or magical techniques, it would be fair to say that you are engaged in a gentle to-and-fro with mysterious forces.

I would argue that there is value in investigating possibility in order to request what you want, rather than writing down a shopping list of outcomes you think will bring you happiness. Otherwise your life will be a patchwork of things, of stuff, rather than experiences; it will be a life of reliance on the external rather than an inward journey of bliss and deep knowing and connection.

If you find yourself curious, but unable to suspend your disbelief, why not give it a try? A bit of gentle conversation with the universe. It can be as simple as writing a list of things you are keen to fulfil or achieve. My only suggestion is to bracket any request with the disclaimer that you receive only if it's in your best interests and does not cause harm to others.

If you really want to make it worthwhile, advance it into an exercise where you deep-dive into why you're seeking those things. What do you perceive as missing from your life? What do you think having those things will do for you? How will they make you feel? How can you feel that way without those things? This is a great way to undertake a quiet, honest appraisal.

It is essential to have a true inner world and sense of being. Stacey Demarco talks about 'the witch's way', which is power from the inside out; others advise to be like the rock in the river that doesn't budge no matter how furious the flow of water. This doesn't mean you should be immoveable; it means, know who you are so that you are not easily led from your intended path.

An abundance of money is unlikely to truly make you happy if your inner world is not abundant and rich in its complexity and meaning. Perhaps it's better to move towards 'tuning in' to intuition, rather than materialistic manifestation. I think this has been my way for years, the rituals and healing modalities just ways to highlight this fact, to bring me into alignment. I wasn't manifesting specific outcomes, I was asking for guidance and opening up to the unexplored possibilities of my life. I was looking for that true spiritual path, the one where your bliss is boundless and not reliant on the world around you. I was interested in gaining a better understanding of the world within. That sounds far more magical to me.

So consider this: manifestation techniques, magic, spells and healing work are not about creating neat outcomes, they are about manifesting your truth. They are steps on an ongoing journey. Such activity and exploration is about finding yourself in the mess of life so that your life reverberates with meaning to you, with a purpose that fulfils you personally, but which hopefully trickles out to benefit the collective in some way. It is about transformation. It is about becoming a creative and fulfilled version of yourself so that you can exist more peacefully in the world.

— CHAPTER SEVEN —

Journeys of Healing

'Let's start healing Amal at every level, especially the base chakra. Sorry, I've just got to do a little bit of plugging into you.'

This is the sort of woo woo thing that awakens my scepticism. But I am in research mode for this book, trying to figure out my own boundaries with the New Age, and like the clinical approach to readings, I decide I need to give 'karmic healing' using crystals a chance. I'm not opposed to what I call 'energetic work', but this is turning out to be bats.

The woman in front of me, let's call her Lumina, is 'plugging in' with me mentally and with crystals, whispering to invisible beings about what needs to be removed. 'Trauma,' she says, eventually. 'I'm getting a bit of trauma that's, and I'm also getting, oh — have you got cysts on your ovaries?'

'No.' No, I don't.

'I'm getting a bit of something around the sacral chakra there.'

We're in a tiny, curtained-off room in the back of a New Age shop. The flimsy 'door' means that a reader's voice pushes through from next door, as does the plucky music from the store, competing with my karmic healer's hushed conversation with my guides. 'It's like you're creating a space for a business . . .'

Lumina continues to whisper. 'I just need Amal's higher self, guardian angel, her guidance systems and structures, and I'm asking that the appropriate healing council show up . . . OK. Thank you so much. So, starting . . .'

Imagery populates my mind as I think of ethereal beings scrambling to assemble on my behalf. What if they were on a break? What if one of them was mid-sandwich when the call came in and he/she/it is all like, 'Can she just get her shit together?'

We only have half an hour so my healer would really like to know if there's anything I would like to work on.

Gosh, where do I begin? I think. A shopping list of issues fills my mind: my tendency to plummet into a bout of low self-esteem as a creative; my self-sabotage mindset; my expertise in self-blame. Am I the problem, like so many New Age and self-help instructors suggest? And, if so, how do I get out of my own way?

Lumina nods. 'I keep going back to these two little points: your soul and your base chakra. So I look at it as really, really old stuff . . . possibly not even this life stuff . . .'

She says some nice things about me — creative, intuitive — before confirming that I'm right: I'm the problem. But soon we're seeing a 'nice shift from the karmic structures'.

Still, there's old stuff. Karmic debt. And she's shoving crystals onto the table, one the size of a granny flat, as she tells me that old and deep stuff is afflicting my current life. It's the same old shit, really, and I start to wonder if that's just why some of this works: most of us are dealing with similar issues. But Lumina interrupts my thoughts by declaring, 'Almost looks Transylvanian.' She doesn't know what that means exactly. Romanian, perhaps?

I don't know what it means either, but before I start imagining a previous life as a vampire, Lumina stutters through more things, peppering her observations with 'I'm not sure', though I'm not sure if it's because she senses my scepticism or because she's just making it all up; or because she's really communicating with invisible beings about my karmic debt.

It starts to take on Kafkaesque proportions.

'It's hard opening and clearing out.' She mutters to herself, confirming vibes and whatnot with 'OK's and 'yeah's. 'This past life thing looks very, very dark . . . so deep and dark and like it's run through generations upon generations . . . but wouldn't it be great if it wasn't there? Wouldn't it be great if we just lighten that up, and wouldn't it be great if we could send something else through there?'

I feel like I'm on a game show and the host is asking me if winning all the prizes would change my life. Why yes, I would like those things, but I have no idea what 'it' is, because I don't know that darkness is fathomable in that way.

Lumina pulls out another crystal to plug me into. She tries to clear ancestral stuff: inherited issues; health problems; the effects of living in the diaspora, of being Palestinian.

'I'm actually seeing a bit of curse action . . . I think it's ancestral. And it's not war-torn Palestine now, it's something else . . . Um, is Romania anywhere near Palestine?'

Healings aren't always this silly. Like readings, they can be useful — if only because they prompt you to consider your own feelings on a matter, or to let go, surrender, transform. But often they are performative like this, drenched in an ostentatious display of 'special' and dripping in New Age speak. The person leading you through will put on a show, hamming up who they are connecting to, cold-reading while they bury you in spiritual props. They will invoke ancient ideas, parrot scientific-sounding terms and make you feel like it's being channelled especially for you.

You will know when something is genuinely moving you, when something is a cathartic experience, even if it's not an outright healing one. Group work can be very energetic and cleansing. Meditation can help to release or clarify. And, of course, people seek out readers and mediums to give them messages that will allow them to move forward in life, away from trauma or pain.

I know that even when I am interested in something, I'm not necessarily convinced it is doing anything except helping me to focus. Sometimes I discover things later —

maybe yoga really does release trauma and emotion? When I did Patty Kikos' Kundalini e-courses, I realised after I had completed the throat chakra e-course (40 days of Kundalini yoga and writing and other activities), that I was singing again. I had stopped at some point. I had honest conversations with people I had worried about for ages; I even noticed that my throat wasn't itchy anymore, so I wasn't doing this strange guttural click that annoys the shit out of everyone.

A true sceptic will tell you that it's confirmation bias. This is often where my scepticism muddles my thoughts. I want to embrace an outcome, but I wonder, am I just creating a truth? After all, two people can see a single event through different lenses and think their idea of it is the only truthful one. But what keeps me here in general, in this space of self-improvement and spiritual experience, is a knowing that overtakes the doubt: I *know* I had an experience when my emotional state changed during a ritual, or doing that Kundalini yoga pose. It happened, even if I can't prove it or accept wholesale what others say it means.

When it comes to transformative work, what I look at is: has something shifted or changed? Can I see something more clearly? Do I have a way forward where previously I felt stuck? It can be as simple as, I feel better, lighter, healed, refreshed, clearer. I didn't just notice these changes directly after doing the throat chakra e-course; I remembered the experiences each morning and how certain positions would change my emotional state. It's not about miraculous healing. This sort of work takes effort, and time. There is power in finding methods you find appealing (and therefore want to invest time in), and in ritualising any kind of personal evolution. It gives it shape and structure, and a changed emotional state is what facilitates change. If you are just feeling 'normal' and like yourself, you are unlikely to be moved.

Patty Kikos works as a wedding celebrant, counsellor and social worker, and says she has a natural affinity with people and a genuine desire to teach, which she does as a senior teacher of both Kundalini and Hatha yoga. She holds a diploma of spiritual healing, is a Reiki master and a kinesiologist.

'*Kundalini* — the word itself means potential,' explains Patty. 'It's raising and expanding your potential, which is just like growth expansion, learning, transcending. But it's about utilising the tools that are already within us because energy healing and yoga philosophy suggest that what we need is already within us. We don't really need that coffee, we don't really need that relationship, we don't really need that degree. Instead, it's about clearing what is unhealed so we can integrate our lessons and embody our gifts.'

I first happened upon Patty when sub-editing an article in a magazine about insurance, where she talked about her home business. I was fascinated by the healing work she described and filed her away in my mind. When she popped up on social media, I decided to pay her a visit. Years later, we are friends. I'm not a regular; that's not the point of Patty's work.

'Kundalini is based on the science of angles and triangles, which means that it stimulates aspects of your nervous system or your glandular system to clear,' Patty explains, 'so that you're able to feel better after clearing whatever blockage was there.'

Kundalini yoga isn't about contortion, like those bikini-clad yoga teachers on Instagram. When you've practised Kundalini yoga for a while, you can hold positions for much longer, instead of shaking involuntarily, which indicates your nervous system is adjusting, says Patty. 'And the idea is that if you strengthen your sensory responses, you're better equipped to deal with life stress. Ideally we want to have enough energy in our reserve tank for when things suddenly go wrong, because it's always the element of surprise that will shock and deplete our system.'

It has helped in Patty's personal life. She can still experience stress, but also recovers quickly. She doesn't want to be in a body that has adjusted to stress so much that it doesn't distinguish between its low and high levels.

Still, Patty is aware that her own healing is an ongoing journey. 'I think that we are eternally healing and I'm an eternal student because I'm a seeker — it's one of my archetypes. I'll always be seeking, learning, growing, expanding.'

Every industry has its crooks, but the MBS field is always under scrutiny, particularly given the vulnerability of its consumer base. But Patty doesn't concern herself with the antagonism.

'If someone wants to share a bad experience, I shut it down,' she says. 'I'm not interested in hearing it because there's always going to be a plumber who did a shit job on your toilet, there's always going to be an electrician who shafted you . . .'

Maybe the word 'healing' is the problem. It suggests the miraculous, and most people don't believe in miracles. In the real world, healing can simply mean the end of pain or trauma; something no longer has power over you, no longer troubles you. But like the knotted skin of a scar, some things will never be forgotten.

Jasmine Hawkins is a full-time healer of the psychic surgery kind. In person, she is radiant. Bright eyes, a sweet smile and softly spoken, she tells me she's a catalyst for change in certain people at particular times. 'I don't need to be the one thing that they always come to, but I'm aware that their soul has contracted me to channel the healing on that day. Then on a different day they could go to the beach and have the same effect. They didn't need me on that day.'

On her website, Jasmine offers an 'instant healing' with an image of a beach.

'It's about taking yourself there, and using your imagination to connect to the elements. Some people who have seen me for a while associate connecting to me with connecting to wisdom, so they might imagine talking to me or being healed by me, but actually it's their own inner being that's responding and making changes.'

Jasmine practically guffaws at the idea of being a 'miracle worker'. She's just a channel. We are our own healers. 'And you cannot force healing or change onto anyone. They have to always allow that to occur.'

I reflect on my first meeting with her, questioning but curious following the recommendation of a friend. I immediately liked Jasmine and found it easy to relax and open up to her. Working with her is an example of where my scepticism gets put to rest and I just feel compelled; I can't explain why it works for me, or if I just think it does, but I have faith that Jasmine is assisting me to clear things. At one point in my first healing, she rested her hands above my head and sat there for minutes in a kind of psychic tete-a-tete with my ancestors. 'I'm asking them for permission,' she told me, because I had come in at a challenging time in my life. My inner sceptic skidded onto the scene . . . Did I really need them to sign a cosmic permission slip to #livemybestlife? Jasmine insisted ancestry was a factor in my life progress, and that women across the board, across all cultures, carry an energy of female suppression.

I forgot about it, until months later, I realised that opportunities I had previously sought out, that required me to be 'seen', were suddenly viable. So now, I ask: 'Do you think it's ultimately the power of the mind?'

'The mind has a lot of power over what we choose, and I do think that our soul can intervene as well. So I think you can be headstrong and try to create things with your mind and that can work to a degree. But if your soul decides to overstep and say, "Nah, that's not happening," it can make forks in the road appear.'

We talk about the power of crystals as talismans. The injection of energy, the gravity of intention. When you light a candle, you're centring your energy. You're declaring that you have a request, and it's a ritual, a spell. All those candles you can find in homewares stores with motivational words and quotes would work in this way. When you light a candle declaring, say, 'gratitude', if you centred yourself and had that intention, it would be like conducting a little spell.

'I think there's a oneness aspect to all beings and all things,' says Jasmine, including crystals. By 'oneness' she means 'consciousness', that mysterious field of energy we connect to as spiritual beings. We, too — our souls — are oneness, as are deities. 'There's this one consciousness, which is experiencing all things at all times,' says Jasmine. We have an illusion of separation because we experience life as an individual. 'But if we break it down to the smallest components, you and I are identical in our consciousness,' Jasmine explains. 'When you call on different beings to ask for help, you're accessing that oneness in whatever form. So if you hold a crystal and think, *Ahhh, now I understand what I have to do*, you can give that power to the crystal and say, "Oh, the crystal told me what to do." To me, it's the oneness.'

BY THE POWER OF CRYSTALS

Essential oils and supplements can get poked and prodded for the healing claims purveyors make about their qualities, but in the ridicule often directed at the New Age, few things draw as much mockery as healings and crystals (and linking the two is the stuff of naysayer fodder).

I get it. There is a lot I have raised my eyebrows at (and still do), but I hope I have never been mean-spirited in my criticism of the New Age. I genuinely don't want to judge someone's choices if it works for them, though as I said earlier, I do wonder at the sheer volume of ways humans choose to heal and transform. And I can't help it: some things do lead to a wry grin and an eye roll when it strikes me as disingenuous or showy (I'm only human).

I think crystals get picked on in part because of their ubiquity: they are fashionable now, easily found in New Age shops but also in chain stores. At one Australian women's clothing retailer, I find crystal kits, packaged in a box with instructions on how to 'cleanse' them. This essentially means clearing the crystals of any negative energy, which crystal diehards can do in a variety of ways — leave them outside to bathe under a full moon; 'reiki' them; sage them; wash them with special water (or just under a tap).

As I've already discussed, New Age spirituality is a trend, evidenced in the highly commercial way it is delivered to the masses. I believe that the more 'glamourised' and possession-focused #spirituality is, the less it truly is spiritual. Tools and props should serve a purpose, not just look good in your Instagram photos. Certainly, crystals are photogenic; they are often beautiful, so they have an aesthetic value that sees people not attuned to mystical aspects decorating their homes and other spaces with them.

I don't look at crystals or any objects as holding inherent mystical or energetic qualities. I don't buy into crystals as being able to heal illness or cure a troubled mind on their own. (Please don't shove a Yoni egg up your hoo-ha.) However, I personally use stones decoratively and as talismans. My writing space is littered with stones. I have them for lots of reasons, but for every project I undertake, I have at least one crystal that symbolises the project for me. And I generally know which ones I want because I'll feel drawn to them.

In the inner west suburb of Glebe in Sydney, tucked between cafés, rests Mineralism, a gem store. From a distance it looks like any crystal shop, crammed with colourful stones, ornaments, jewellery display cases and a handful of books and card decks. But its point of difference is who runs it: Jed Underwood, a quietly spoken American, and his wife, Jess Lahoud, a Lebanese-Australian woman with a beatific smile. Both are passionate about crystals, and the store, which is in its fourth year, is gaining a large following on social media and in person. Jed and Jess are at its heart, but even when they're not there you'll find beaming staff ready to direct you to the right crystal.

I don't want to sound like an advertisement. I'm just a fan, and a somewhat regular customer. I call Jed my 'crystal whisperer' because he always knows what I need before I do. He prescribes stones like a gentle pharmacist for the soul. When I was struggling with the draft of a challenging book, I wandered through his store, heavy and uncertain. He strolled over and held out a collection of gemstones. He held up each stone and explained its suitability, identifying succinctly the issues I faced writing about ageing and illness: seraphinite, for healing, because of the personal journey I'd gone through; fluorite, for clarity and getting things done; pyrite, for energy; sunstone, for happiness. For this book: an egg-shaped piece of polished red jasper — good for grounding, but also useful when you have a lot of information to distil (ha!) and have to be selective (a small kind of torture for someone like me, who wants to cover all bases).

Jed could hand me anything, but the most valuable element is what he says. Kind of like a mini reading, if you will.

I tell him what I call him when we meet on a sunny weekday morning to have a chat for this book. He chuckles at the title. Jed is good-natured, thoughtful in his speech. So when I ask him where we even begin with crystals — an area that is fraught with misconception, doubt and cynicism — he is ready to offer a fresh perspective.

'The easiest way to break it down in the first place would be to consider a quartz crystal. If you throw it at the street as hard as you can in the pitch black of night, it's not going to hit the street and just break. You'll see an explosion within the quartz as it hits, you'll see a spark ignite. And then it will explode and pop into pieces . . . So to see that the stones have an energy to them is . . . that's the most simple way.'

Quartz grows inside the earth, Jed continues. 'In the same way we grow on this earth, Mother Nature, there's energy that goes into the stone. You can take it and use it and look at it in so many different ways,' he says. Then you ask some questions: 'What do I feel from this energy? Am I creating this feeling of this energy because so many have told me this is the energy of the stone?'

Jed says crystal meanings are a mixed bag, though. Consider the history of crystals, of how they have been used. Invented meanings have stuck to the stone for years.

There are numerous books and card decks that offer crystal meanings, promises of healing and wisdom associated with traditional practices. They exhaustively detail how to get your crystals, how to use them for healing and how to cleanse them. The latter is considered especially important because users of crystals tend to believe they don't simply provide energy, they also absorb it.

JOURNEYS OF HEALING

Some stones have meanings that seem to be universally agreed upon: clear quartz is a master crystal — an amplifier of any other stone, and a cleanser of them, too. Amethyst is a stone of intuition; black tourmaline offers protection, and rose quartz, in all of its heartwarming soft pink, is considered the 'love stone'. I've gifted rose quartz to friends before — it's a nice one for gentle connection because of its look, but I also pack it with an intention for the person.

Jed looks for meaning beyond the colour of a stone, and he gets feedback from people. He talks to, say, a hundred people a month, who communicate that they truly feel the energy of a gemstone. 'I've talked to maybe 25 different people that can hold a piece of rose quartz and say, "Yes, I feel that it has a strong love energy to it, and I feel that in my heart." In saying that, I've also talked to probably just as many people who say, "I pick it up. I feel nothing from it. It's cool. It's a beautiful thing that grew in the earth, but I don't feel an energy coming off of it."'

I suggest that why anything works is because of the common denominator of 'you', the person using the crystal or doing a practice.

'In one way the crystal can be a healing crystal, and can affect us and can help us without having any energy to it at all, because we put that intention into it. Every time we touch it, it reminds us that we need to work on that thing within us. In that way, it can also be thought of as a placebo because it's something that certain people won't believe has any energy to it.'

Jed is a pretty chill kind of guy. He's been working in the industry since he was six years old, literally. His mother ran a stall at a flea market, so Jed would help load and unload the trucks of a wholesale gem and mineral company. He's like Patty, who isn't too bothered with proving things to the masses. He knows his audience, and to the ones who enter with doubt and curiosity, he still offers his full attention.

'I've also been around people who do it in a very different way and will push things on people and say, "You need this for this reason. I see that you look fatigued. You need to have this pyrite to bring up your energy, and you will be a happier person if you have this stone in your life."

'And I get very frustrated . . . This is my livelihood and my passion. I love gemstones. I love the amazing things that come out of the earth, and I've seen them truly help people.'

Jed hates seeing crystals mass-produced and sold in chain stores. 'The employees who work there know nothing about it. They couldn't tell you the name of the stone if they picked it up and it didn't have it written on it. They sell it as a healing kit, but they have absolutely no clue what it does, how it works.'

We talk about Instagram, where things are shiny and where people often showcase a life not really being lived. And those drink bottles with gems in them? Jed looks genuinely pained at the #crystalelixir trend.

I point out that stones can be porous and it's therefore #dangerous.

'It's one of the reasons I don't sell the gem bottles,' Jed says. 'There're a few companies here in Sydney that make them, and the stones that they use are actually dangerous to have in your water.'

They're meant to transform the water into some sort of magical elixir. They're on trend, with certain celebrities leading the charge. They can be expensive, too, with consumers paying between $100 and $500. One of the stones commonly used is labradorite, Jed notes, which has an aluminium base. 'So if you drink out of a water bottle that's been soaking in that labradorite, it can bring toxins into your body that you're not used to, and you're bringing a heavy metal into your body without even thinking about it. And these people that have no knowledge of what crystals do, what their make-up is, what their chemical breakdown is, are selling these stones as healing stones, but they don't have any clue what you do with them, how you use them.'

Is it all about making money? To me, it seems increasingly about the *appearance* of a life infused with wellness. I wonder how much of our personal journeys is a curated presentation of those things rather than a genuine authentic experience of them. It's quite troubling.

'We deal with that surface stuff so much more than we deal with things that are truly going on within us,' Jed says. 'I feel like, in today's society, we get lost in what I call internet shamanship.' A quick quiz and a printed certificate qualifies you as a crystal healer. '[They are saying] "I'm ready to heal you and take care of you," yet they have no truth, no experience, no true light to what they believe.'

It's also disrespectful to traditional shamanism, I say.

'Yeah, absolutely. I grew up in New Mexico, and I grew up spending a lot of time on . . . the Navajo and Santo Domingo Pueblo, and a lot of the different Indian Pueblos.

I spent a lot of time learning how they use crystals. How they clear their crystals, how they pick their sage. You know, you go up the mountain singing this song of cleansing and clearing yourself, and then you pick the sage and you come down the mountain singing a song, thanking the earth for giving you that sage for cleansing.'

Jed describes a difficult life, but he feels blessed to have spent time with Native Americans. This, he emphasises, doesn't qualify him as a shaman. 'You have to study under a Native American shaman for twenty years before you can even consider yourself a shaman in the Native American culture.'

In his book *Crystals and the New Age*, Stuart Weinberg says crystals in this market emerged in the 1980s. There were rock shops, but occult bookstores 'morphed into New Age gift shops with books'. Books were a challenge to make profitable in a widening marketplace, while crystals offered 'retail-friendly' profit margins for metaphysical stores.

The New Age as a retail proposition was changing. 'The New Age pragmatized the Mineral Kingdom,' says Weinberg. Healing modalities and the like integrated crystals, and there was a revival in traditions that used them. Miners paid attention. A new market for stones was opening up. A rising focus on chakras, astrology and channelling helped build a commercial crystal industry.

This is something that arises in my conversation with Jed. He appears extremely ethical: I once asked him about a particular stone and he told me he doesn't have it — he won't buy it. Too hard to get the real thing. He shares examples of vendors peddling fake stones, especially more valuable ones like moldavite, what Jed says is a 'beautiful, high vibrational stone'.

And what of the unethical ways stones are often sourced? Ravaging the earth to mine stones we have no right to? Jed says he is mindful of where his stones come from. 'Because I'm selling them to people as healing stones, stones with good energy behind them, you never want to find out that somebody sent a little kid up the mountain to go dig these stones out, and the kid never learned how to go to school because he was forced into the mining world and never had the opportunity to live life and find his way through this.

'There're also people who will drill a hole in the side of a mountain and put a stick of dynamite in and blow up half of a mountain just to find little bits of quartz crystal in that mountain. Maybe they make $500 off of blowing up a mountain, but they're so focused on the money of it that they're not figuring out what they're doing to the planet.'

Jed is strict about sourcing: he won't buy them cheaply and wholesale if the vendor can't tell him the history behind it. 'Everything in my shop, I can tell you the name of the miner that found it. I can tell you what area it was found in, because we've made really good friends with the different miners all around the world. And I've been doing this for so long, since I was a little kid, that I can walk around and see these different miners, and we know each other by name and we give each other a big hug and call each other brother.

'I know people from all different religions, all different walks of life, and they find these gemstones and they dig them up and they make a livelihood for their family, or even for their whole village. And so most of my Moroccan fossils and stuff will come from one village in Morocco, and I know that I can buy them cheaper from one of the big wholesalers, but instead I would like to buy them from this village . . .'

Jed went there in his first year of business and placed an order. He was told that the money the miner made from the supply would go to supporting the village for a year.

He doesn't want to be like other foreigners going into a country to ravage its natural resources. 'Instead, I stand so strongly in buying from the people that are from that land, who have this strong love and belief for their country,' he says. Jed explains that many of the miners he works with will trek into the mountains with a backpack and spend a week digging up crystals. He is moved by the beauty of their connection with nature.

In my experience, people who use crystals are no stranger than a performer who has a pre-show ritual, or someone who insists that they wear a pair of lucky underwear when they play a footy match. Have you ever bought a piece of jewellery and mentally charged it with personal symbolism? It's the same idea with crystals. They are pretty, nice to look at and hold, and can act as a tool to focus your thoughts or understand your emotions. Some might call this the placebo effect, but what is that really but a person exercising their will and using their powerful mind?

You're probably wondering if any object could have served that purpose then, right? A ruler? A piece of paper? A mouse pad?

Well, maybe. But a mouse pad doesn't really provoke an inward slide into a clearer mind. It holds no spiritual value for me. Also, I would look ridiculous massaging a mouse pad. A mouse pad has utility, not emotional resonance.

Finding something that you can connect to is the key.

COLOUR

I arrive at Claire Hickson's flat on a chilly Sunday afternoon for a session of Aura-Soma, a modality that employs colour to deep dive into oneself. Claire is an independent practitioner, and she is my go-to when I need some clarity or a tune-up. Sitting in her home office, I take in more than a hundred little hypercolour bottles lined up in a large light box display.

Aura-Soma is, literally, a colourful experience. The bottles, containing liquids in various shades of colour, are made up of oil, crystals, herbs and water. Your reader will invite you to select four, and then use them to provide insight into your life. It's been years since I first tried it, propelled towards warm-hearted Claire after a failed attempt at a do-it-yourself Aura-Soma reading online. It turns out, a face-to-face session is infinitely better. Having an experienced reader means you can have a conversation and go deeper than a miniscule online interpretation.

Today, I'm here as a storyteller, interested in doing a stocktake of Aura-Soma for this book. I'm at a turning point in my life, coming to terms with shifting beliefs and ideas, my malleability and open mind no longer a burden but an asset.

The last time I saw Claire was when I was writing a book on ageing and illness, exploring my own journey with it, and I was flatlining, defeated. I have always been a curious person but being confronted with so many stories of pain, sadness and loss, I was adrift, and I sought out Claire to help me rebalance. To help me write, because I was staring at my book from a distance, unable to assemble it.

And it worked. 'You're experiencing shock every time you hear someone's story, and rather than getting rid of it, you absorb it and now it has snuck up on you,' she told me then, gently as always.

The Aura-Soma colour system is a unique practice that encompasses well-known spiritual components, developed by Vicky Wall, an English surgical podiatrist who lost her eyesight. Colours are relevant in certain modalities, particularly cards and crystals. Aura-Soma takes it a step further by creating meaning from the colours, which are made from semi-precious stones, gems and crystals.

'It's a liquid, but it's the energy of the crystals that goes in through a tincture. So if you have yellow, for example, and orange, there might be calcified citrine in there. Red has ruby and green has emerald.'

The liquids also contain essential oils from plants grown on a biodynamic farm in the UK, according to the moon cycles. 'Everything is done with intention.'

Looking at the hypercolour bottles, they look anything but natural, but I've always found Aura-Soma to be a fascinating examination into self. Like card decks, rituals and crystals, it has taught me that it's not the action alone that matters, but the intention you bring to it.

Intention is everything in spirituality. It sits at the core of manifestation principles (what you put out you attract);

it's a foundation of any act of prayer and worship; and is even a component of spells for the magically inclined.

It is arguably the modality I am the least cynical about because it is not prescriptive. Sure, it has its woo woo elements — ascended masters, *I Ching*, tarot and archangels make up part of its architecture. Yet none of these are essential to the process. The times that I have worked with Aura-Soma, I've been amazed at how it can feel like going on a journey. It's the best kind of transformation because it's the sort of change that sneaks up on you, and at the heart of it all is you making those shifts, doing the 'shadow' work and figuring out stuff for yourself.

I was first introduced to Aura-Soma years ago when I was working in the city. Whenever I passed by Wynyard station, I would notice a poster featuring a series of colourful bottles, often two colours in one, separated like oil on water. I resisted my curiosity at first, never feeling inclined to visit the psychic upstairs. But my curiosity sprouted wings and led me to an online app and a minor existential crisis of colour.

While Aura-Soma does involve chance in that you select bottles based on feeling, it is not fatalistic like tarot or oracle cards. You are attracted to certain bottles, and each one has a message. In a session, you select four, each one representing a state: the first, your soul bottle; the second, gifts and talents (challenges); the third, your present situation; the fourth, the future. It is not oracular in the traditional sense, but it is a useful tool in uncovering the hidden, possibly grimy parts of yourself that you have comfortably kept tucked away.

At the end, you are encouraged to 'work with' a bottle.

'It is a tool for understanding and healing yourself,' says Claire. 'It is really important that we don't call it a "healing tool" [as this] suggests that it is doing something [miraculous]. We don't say that. However, if you're choosing to heal yourself, you can use Aura-Soma as a tool. It's an energetic tool. And the reason why it's important no one holds or shakes your bottle is because it has your energy in it.'

When I pick my bottles, Claire carries them by the lid. The bottle has its own 'energy', and it becomes yours. It's working with you. The colours can even change depending on who is using the bottle, she says.

'And it's a tool that can bring great relief,' continues Claire, adding that it can work at another level when combined with counselling or other practices, such as massage. 'It's like an amplifier that you connect your guitar to.'

Claire always puts out a box of tissues before a session. It's not so much ominous as wise. Tears are not unusual. Claire is highly empathetic. She is warm, speaks in a soft, English-accented voice, and oozes kindness. If you start to cry, she will, too. But she doesn't grandstand her empathy; the moment and space remains yours, despite her insanely intuitive responses.

As your guide in Aura-Soma, Claire is not here to judge, or even tell you what to do. She chaperones you on what can be a joyful or perilous journey, depending on your outlook.

For the first time in years, I ask Claire why Aura-Soma 'works' for me. I have my own intuitive sense of it, but I'm curious about the official party line.

'We are on our own path,' begins Claire. 'And the beauty of Aura-Soma is it is connected to ancient wisdom systems. And we are the sum of our past, whether we believe in past lives or not. Even if we don't, it's from the point of our conception to birth to where we are now. There's a timeline.'

The colours look at the collection of your experiences. But also, Claire explains, the past, present and future are all connected, which means we're carrying with us our ancestors' stories.

In a session, as the client you do most of the talking. But Claire interprets the meaning of a bottle and, more importantly, its connection to you. She says a session will only ever do what a person is open to; for example, if you are deeply religious and worry about doing this kind of practice, the session will reflect your ideology and situation.

As for the bottles, Claire gives an example of how one would work. 'If a woman is having an issue with her mother, for example, she may choose a bottle that is representative of all the things that really frustrate her about her mother, but actually, it's part of herself, too.'

In other words, the thing you think is the problem is usually masking a deeper issue. 'The journey never ends in any particular issue. However, you can find resolution with it, and a peace with it.'

In today's session, I find myself hesitating before I make my picks, second-guessing myself, perhaps more aware of how it all works. But Aura-Soma still holds some mystery for me, unlike cards with a reader, where I have to resist the instinct to read them myself. At some point, I learned to trust my own intuition more than that of the readers. But here, I am in Claire's able hands.

I sheepishly tell Claire that I picked a bottle second but put it in the third spot. She stops short of clucking at me and gently moves the bottles around so that they are in the order I selected them.

Today's reading, not surprisingly, reflects my current state. My first bottle, the soul one, contains dark red over deep blue. It's the 'get up and go' bottle, Claire tells me. It's about discernment in where I put my energy. 'The stillness of the blue offering peace and standing in your own natural authority.'

The second and third bottles — gifts and talents, and the present — are 'archangel bottles', which Claire thinks is rather significant. Having two in one reading, that is. The second bottle is magenta and olive, though it looks more pale green. 'It makes me think of a watermelon,' I tell Claire, and she laughs. 'Love comes in letting go' is the affirmation for this bottle, which tells me to see the bigger picture but also pay attention to the finer details. It heralds divine love coming through and shining light on who I am, says Claire. 'Green showing your heart, hope and courage — your way, your truth, your life.'

The 'what's happening now' bottle is a mid-turquoise/pale green one that has shifted to look mostly light blue. It speaks of letting go of the past. 'Showing your creativity, stepping into your own path of individuation, speaking your truth and expressing who you are.'

Then the future bottle. Claire lights up. I have selected the wisdom bottle, 'El Dorado'. It's gold over gold, the top half transformed to pale gold.

'I see in front of me the gold at the end of the rainbow. My whole being fills with light. That's the affirmation,' says Claire, like a proud school teacher. 'Connecting with your wisdom and sharing it with the world, leadership, shining your light out into the world. Filling your cup so you can give to others.'

As mentioned earlier, it's been years since I first began working with Claire, and it occurs to me that she would see me differently from how I see myself. I grow curious in our meeting. As we wrap up, I query Claire on working with me all these years.

'How have I changed since I first started coming to you?' I say, truly unsure about what Claire might say. (It will be very nice, of course, because it's Claire and she is incapable of being unkind. Still. I'm vulnerable.)

'Well, what I remember about you and what I see in you now is the person that came to me was very questioning and . . . There was something in you that knew there was something in Aura-Soma for you.'

So far, so nice. But then Claire continues: 'I remember you struggling with trying to adapt to living in this culture with a really strong family background of your religion.'

She reminds me that I gave her a copy of my first novel, *Courting Samira*, a humorous take on being single and Muslim in your twenties (it's chick-lit, all right?), and how I had hoped that it would offer insight into why I was so screwed up when it came to love: self- and otherwise (my words, not hers).

'I loved that book . . . and you had this person who liked you [my now-husband Chris] and you kind of liked them but there was this difficulty with your family, and then suddenly, as time progressed, you were getting married to this person and I was so happy for you. And what I've seen is this growing confidence with bringing both of those aspects together in terms of your upbringing and where you live and the culture that you're living in now.'

Nothing Claire says here should be surprising or seem new, and yet I realise how distant that version of me is now. How far I have come. How much I have forgotten about the straddling of two worlds that for so long was my 'normal'.

I think the thing that's changed for me is accepting my parents for who they are, and not needing them to change for me; I will change but they don't have to. When I'm with them, I can just be their daughter.

I am someone, I have realised over the years, who likes the physicality of journeys towards 'healing'. I need action and relish ritual. I sit in my head enough; enacting change is essential to my growth, even if it's symbolised in a bottle.

Like anything I have used to broker change in myself and my life, Aura-Soma is a tool. It's in my kit. It's not a solution for everything; it's an insightful mechanism I can use to settle and balance aspects of my life. And while the woo woo aspects don't bother me, I would say a full-time sceptic might struggle with its architecture of ascended masters and archangels.

For me, it's an example of where I can work with a system that appeals to me (pretty colours!), with the right person (Claire is wonderful), to clarify what's happening in my world. After all, anything you do requires a suspension of disbelief because in your ordinary state, most, if not all of this, makes no sense. But when you ritualise, create a structure, and change your emotional state, you let go of intellect and allow for insight. It's like an exhalation.

Perhaps I can best explain it by saying, you could probably get similar results through different practices, but like the vehicle you use to get you from A to B, some things make for a better experience based on your personal tastes and preferences. I love otherworldly things, and transcending the ordinary, but I try to make it useful and transformative, and I select with care the vehicles I use to take me there.

My best advice to anyone seeking spiritual or mystical nourishment is to do the same. Experiment, enjoy, but also be discerning in how you expend your time and energy.

JUST DANCE . . .

The story of how self-conscious me decides to participate in conscious dance begins in Beirut, Lebanon. It's a sunny day in September when I sit opposite Nikita Shahbazi, an Iranian woman living in the Middle East, who dances her way through refugee camps and helps people to unfurl through her IMOVE Foundation. She's here to share with me how dancing has helped her, and now others, to heal.

A survivor of the Iraq–Iran war in the 1980s, Nikita fled with her family to Europe in the 1990s. 'And besides that, my family were persecuted during the Islamic Revolution. I am a Muslim but we were quite liberal and I would say they were in the opposition during the regime of the Shah and they were leftists. So after the revolution they had to leave. Most of our friends and my sister had to leave the country, and my brother was arrested for a while.'

Nikita is a softly spoken woman in her forties. She describes a turbulent childhood, with a depressed mother and a volatile father (who, she says, was also rebellious and taught her to not follow the herd). The trauma of her difficult childhood remained in her body, she says, when she arrived in the Netherlands at sixteen years old. She is thoughtful but knowing as she talks about how she addressed the resulting post-traumatic stress through dance, yoga and meditation.

'I needed tools in order to become resilient and process what I had been through in my previous years,' she tells me when we meet on a bright morning in Beirut.

I'm in Lebanon to interview women for a book that explores the lives of Arab women, and I'd found an event on Facebook that Nikita was running in Beirut — a 5Rhythms dance session, a form of conscious dance created by the now-deceased dancer Gabrielle Roth that has a global fan base. Nikita is training to teach classes, but in the meantime runs conscious or free dancing and movement sessions for refugees.

'What 5Rhythms does is basically bring you in touch with your emotions through a wave, a phase of five kinds of different music,' Nikita explains. 'You will express your emotions, release them and transfer them into dance.'

In order, the 'five rhythms' of the wave are: flowing, staccato, chaos, lyrical and stillness. A session normally runs for a couple of hours, but Nikita provides a simpler offering to the refugees she works with, limiting sessions to one hour of mindful dancing, as a mindfulness trainer.

She combines mindfulness exercises to bring them into contact with their feelings, discomfort and memories.

'It is a meditative dance. You are dancing with your thoughts; you are dancing with your emotion. It's not a dance for beauty, it's not a dance for performing, it is more putting your power, putting your thoughts, putting your feelings into dance. Discovering who you are and shedding off all the masks, all the wounds of the war, traumas, what [you] have been through.'

The women Nikita guides require a lot of instruction. 'It's not easy for them to get in touch with their emotions and let their emotions move . . . It's too heavy emotionally.' But it can also be rewarding because 'it is you who interprets who you want to be or how you want to act and what emotions come out'.

It has an element of connection with the divine beyond and within us. That was Roth's intention, Nikita says, to make dance in the West spiritual, inspired also by shamans in the US, adding the element of awareness, grounding, being who you are.

5Rhythms has been the most transformative technique for Nikita, who does it often; but it is only one aspect of her healing, which began in the Netherlands, a country that 'gives you a lot of space to develop your own identity'. Nikita took dance classes, she did yoga, and more, in order to recover and find ways to cope with life's daily challenges.

'I mean it was not an easy thing, learning a new language at that age, getting used to a different education system, which I never finished because I really couldn't get used to it.'

Although Nikita didn't finish high school, she still

attended university. But she found her path in movement and dance. 'I really need them to get in touch with myself. It helped me a lot.' Compared to how others in her situation have fared, she says movement has made her stronger and more positive. 'This was the medicine for my emotions, for my mental life in order to remain positive. Because once you have been through a war, you are not the same person anymore.' Your whole existence, as a witness to war and persecution, is fear-based, says Nikita.

'So I was aware that I had to do something about it, because in every decision in my life, especially every private and important decision, it was fear that popped up in my head. You always think that you're going to lose and it's going to be nothing and this is the worst thing that you can do. I mean, how can I explain it? Your whole existence is based on negativity and avoiding fear and avoiding the worst situation.'

Nikita says her own experiences and those of other women she has worked with confirmed the link between mind, body and spirit: 'The women who were always active, physically active and busy with their minds and body, they were more in control over their lives.'

Nikita explored the impact of dancing, yoga, mindfulness and empowerment (i.e. having choice). The results confirmed for Nikita a correlation between activity and empowerment. 'And this made me inspired to set up my own foundation for spreading the healing of mindfulness and dancing.'

When Nikita saw the influx of Syrian refugees, she knew where her focus should lie: helping people — children and women especially — heal from their traumas.

When we meet, it's been a couple of years since she began, and Nikita says women are extremely receptive to her work. 'It's incredible. I am so sorry because I am not able to cover or target more women . . . Their bodies are full of tension and fear. They are burdened. The way you move, the way you sit, the way you behave — your body tells all your biography, your story, your social conditioning.'

Even science will agree: post-traumatic stress disorder (PTSD), the kind someone who has lived through or participated in war might experience, can have severe mental and physical effects. It might go some way to explaining how some New Age thinkers link illness to our mental and emotional states.

But how far do you take that? If we can store trauma in our bodies, can we inherit it from our ancestors? The field of epigenetics explores the inheritance of transgenerational trauma. Some say the verdict is still out on this, but discussion around this centres on the biological memory of trauma. The New Age is less circumspect — it traffics heavily in ancestral inheritance.

I don't *love* conscious dance in any form, truth be told. I've done various forms of it. But I must admit it has helped me to unpack my troubled relationship with my body, with being a woman. I wrote about it for a Women of Letters event at the Sydney Opera House, then later for *frankie* magazine. I can poke fun at myself and the space, and the dramatic dancing. But I am also filled with admiration for the people who come and have zero fucks to give about how they look when they dance.

Later, when I'm in the US, I decide to seek out a class run by Jo Cobbett, whom I'd met at a weekend dance course in Sydney a couple of years before, a gentle woman in her sixties who is proof that dance is good for your body, mind and soul.

'Dance' for Jo is an embodied type of dance rather than a dictatorial one. 'I'm unfortunately not so fond of the systems where it's an imposed sense of order and then there's a certain amount of freedom within it,' she tells me.

The dance preceding our conversation sees a small group of people of diverse backgrounds converge on a Masonic hall. As is common with this sort of dance event, there is an altar. Today, Jo has set up two small wooden mannequins with a red ribbon between them. The ribbon, Jo explains, is a little thread to start with as dancers connect and reach out to each other. 'And how much more can there be?'

I am, as always, self-conscious. But I like Jo's energy, and the space she facilitates. She has trained in a number of different modalities, but today's session is an open floor exploration. She plays some Joni Mitchell because it's her birthday. At one point, she asks us to partner up: this doesn't have to involve touch, but arguably it requires connection. I get a guy called Jorge and I think I'm a difficult partner. Have you ever tried looking a stranger in the eye and not looking away immediately? Now try doing that while freestyle-dancing.

Jo calls it 'witnessing'. 'Part of the reason I wanted people to have the luxury of witnessing each other is because there's something so exquisitely authentic that happens. It's like you can't really pretend you're somebody else on the dance floor.'

Besides: 'A lot of people don't come in to be conscious in conscious dance. A lot of people come in to be unconscious in conscious dance,' Jo says.

It's a fair point: how is it conscious if the point is abandon? 'Because it's really about abandoning the way the intellect functions for the luxury of entering a level of physicality that's quite different than mind over matter, and I really value mind over matter in so many ways,' explains Jo. 'I value the idea that we are here to inhabit ourselves and also to give ourselves permission to screen out what is not really nourishing for us.'

The emotion work in dance depends on the teacher and how they're teaching it. Jo's style is informed by two different streams of embodied practice. 'I started out meeting Gabrielle Roth one night and then went into a workshop with Emilie Conrad who founded Continuum Movement. They were both pioneers. They both developed their bodies of work at the same time and they started out on fairly similar tracks. They were both dancers.'

Like any meditative process, there was a process of exploration below the surface of things, not asking 'why', but 'what' and 'how'. A series of enquiries into the body. 'How is this going to take me? Where does this unravel me? And just noticing and tracking and tracking and tracking.'

Both Roth and Conrad developed a 'wave'.

'The wave form is our natural flow, it's the way energy moves. It's the way water moves, which we can see.'

Even Vedic tradition, an ancient, non-religious set of teachings and ideas passed down from sages of the Indian sub-continent, speaks of being oceanic, of being waves.

'It's mapping something that already exists. Discovering it for yourself as though for the first time. And in Continuum Movement, when things got slowed down, there was the awareness that the [wave] system worked in the same kind of energetic waves.'

Dance is not my preferred method of shedding stuff. There is something too communal and packed about the space. Too performative. Too raw. I'm essentially just too self-conscious to peel away my layers in this way.

But I can't say I didn't learn anything about myself. The primary lesson is that I don't like such open healing. But I can vouch for the 'energy' that might grow and fill a space when emotions are high. I see through others how much dance means to them, how it has healed and transformed their lives. One man told me he used to be an addict (drugs and alcohol). Dance saved him. A lot of people speak this way about that one thing that really defines them. And for many, conscious dance is a definitive, community-oriented practice.

I felt this most deeply one day at a workshop with Alana Fairchild, author of numerous books and oracle decks. She is kind and has an angelic voice, but she will also play Rage Against The Machine to spur those gathered around her into a heightened state. That particular day, I was in mourning. Months earlier, my aunt on my mother's side had unexpectedly passed away. It hit me hard, and took a while to loosen the shock. But as the group wound themselves into a yelping frenzy to very loud music, something in me broke and I began to cry. Before I knew it, Alana — who was leading us with a microphone — was embracing me. I still found it difficult to completely surrender.

Not sure why. Perhaps it was something to do with my upbringing, where I was raised to be hyper aware of my behaviour as a woman. Or it could be that, as women in modern society, we're punished for being too emotional or too loud. I'm sure there is a lot of stuff around femininity I haven't properly unpacked.

Who knows? I can ask, but really, I simply accept that in that moment, there was connection between strangers, and it was real. Which is why I can say, hand on heart, that while I don't love conscious dance, I absolutely understand why others flock to it.

CREATIVE CATHARSIS

Author Elizabeth Gilbert speaks frequently on the magic of creativity. Her book *Big Magic* unpacks the idea of 'the muse' and how creative work can lead to healing. I have found this to be true in my own experiences; strange manifestations or coincidences in something I write, or an unfurling of something within me, pain losing its edge, or sorrow reshaping itself.

It's perhaps one of the reasons I love card decks so much; each one appears to me a personal journey for both the artist and the writer — a story plays out, a unique energy imprinted on a tool for understanding ourselves better, or for creating a new way forward.

Creativity, while useful and significant for many reasons, is at its heart a form of catharsis, a way to understand ourselves and our world. It is metaphysical, even if you're not a believer.

While my primary creative tool is writing, in recent times, my field has expanded in unexpected but very welcome ways. Which is to say, I am doing stuff I instinctively wanted to do when I was a kid but wasn't allowed to, or didn't succeed at (I would have made a great sidekick in the school play, but whatever).

As someone who does her share of public speaking, I have found it immensely helpful to take up improv theatre. Part of my intention in signing up was to scratch an acting itch, but also to be less afraid of looking like an idiot when speaking in public (I can be very self-conscious at times). It has achieved those goals to be sure. But its positive impact on my wellbeing surprised me. Through it, I have made friends. I found a cool community where I studied, at Improv Theatre Sydney; it's naturally diverse and fun. Improv makes you better at being in the moment, better at listening and lighter after three hours of play.

For my good friend Zeina Iaali, her purification comes through art. She's a high school teacher of the subject and a talented artist herself, and patiently she teaches me about art and why it's so important.

I love everything she does, and among her works are a series of mandalas, which she calls 'meditation illustrations'. When I visit her one evening for dinner, I bring a newly acquired *Art Oracles* deck ('Creative and life inspiration from the great artists'), written by Katya Tylevich, with illustrations by Mikkel Sommer. It's abstract and funky, with vivid depictions of tortured artists and their work, and succinct advice 'drawn from three key elements in their lives'. Namely: life, work and inspiration.

Henri Matisse, for example, stands before a painting and advises to 'Unleash the beast within'. The inspiration: 'Sketch boldly and paint with a big stick.'

It is a striking deck, even for an art noob like myself, who doesn't know her Van Gogh from her Dürer. As I slowly peruse them, I'm struck by the melancholic nature of the lives on display, the way the stories play into each other, and that thread of despairing creativity we so long ago bought as essential. However, these cards offer something more than sadness over a tortured life. It is deeply spiritual: stripping away the façade to reveal the raw, enduring and remarkable truth of you, of situations. Less soothsaying and more life advice, perhaps, but isn't that what oracles are for?

Zeina excitedly shuffles through the cards, explaining the advice on some of them. 'Oh! I just taught the students in my class about Wassily Kandinsky!' she tells me, when he jumps out. ('Transcend systems to find spirit.')

She laughs heartily at Marcel Duchamp, the French-American artist most famous for his conceptual work. On the card, Duchamp stands in a fur coat, arms outstretched, before a men's urinal. 'Making it look easy is hard,' the card's work advice reads before declaring, 'May your bathroom humour leave a serious legacy' (inspiration). Zeina explains this to me: Duchamp's legacy is the readymade artwork — a urinal he named *Fountain*.

I am not an artist or an art aficionado, but I can enjoy it with the right narration. I love stories, and hearing about the meaning or intention of a work has an instant effect on me. Months earlier, Zeina led me through an exhibition of Muslim artists in which she was featured. Her work, 'Sweetly

Moulded' (2012), featured hand-cut Perspex moulds of *mamoul* (a sweet Arabic biscuit) that honour her female lineage, a nod to her Lebanese heritage and the communal activities of women who make these sweets for celebrations.

For Zeina, art is not her source of torture; it is a place of liberation. I sense in her a vibrancy that makes it fulfilling, cathartic and even healing. Years ago, I first saw her precise mandala drawings. She explained that she had asked the question, 'What is love?' before she started to draw.

It all started when she was going through a hard time, she tells me, as we sort through the oracle cards. 'I was feeling upset and I just wanted to free my mind because I love art. It's always been in me, but it's like the pressure of just trying to know what to make, what to do, sometimes it weighs you down. So I wanted to do something where I was just free to do anything. And so I grabbed a pen, a piece of paper and I just said, whatever comes to mind, just do it. It was just a process of letting go.'

Zeina simply wanted to create something, without worrying about an outcome, or about being brilliant.

'I just didn't want to think about it. I wanted it to be almost mind-numbing.' Like a TV show binge. 'I wasn't drawing a picture of a face or an object. I just wanted to do anything. And so it started off with a dot in the middle of the paper.'

'And you would ask questions sometimes, wouldn't you?'

'Yes. It's from the centre working my way out and whatever just came to my mind. So sometimes it's just repeated; a pattern that I just kept repeating, repeating, over and over and over again. And it just calmed me. It gave me something to do. It was like a challenge, almost.'

While Zeina simply wanted to let go and draw, she was surprised by the therapeutic and cathartic nature of the work. This was purely for her, as well, so she hesitated to share the pieces. But they are striking, and I selfishly want them to be seen.

Mandalas are considered healing templates by some; energy is transmitted into them in their creation. The word 'mandala' is a Sanskrit word that literally means 'circle' and as a symbol represents the universe. They are rooted in the traditions of Hinduism and Buddhism.

Nowadays, oracle decks featuring 'energetically channelled' mandalas are common. Rather than simply representing a meaning, they are used in ritual for healing an aspect of your life or yourself. They are not miraculous, nor are they magic pills, but you will find instructions on where to place the mandala (at your feet, against your heart). It's easy to scoff at this sort of thing, but the power of ritual, to me anyway, is the intention and the energy you raise while undertaking it.

The mandala isn't the point; it's like a witch's wand, a place to put the energy you have brewing inside of you; or, if you ranked higher on the woo woo scale, a way to tap into some universal life force energy, one that was used to create an intention for the mandala in the first place. They are frequently used in oracle decks, though you will also find 'activators' these days — images of imaginary or mythological creatures, mandalas and more that have been charged with energy and 'activate' something.

Years ago, when I embarked on my Kundalini yoga with Patty Kikos, her online sessions included mandala creations. I lost myself in them. I would just draw, poorly and without precision or style because I'm not an artist like Zeina, but there would be intention. I would write words around the mandala before I commenced to have a sense of where I would be journeying when I began to draw. And, as with any kind of 'energy work', it's about a letting go, a clarifying and cathartic surrender. A washing away of confusion so that something can be better understood.

Perhaps something manifests as a result of it, but that is not necessarily the intention. It's not magical, it's a distillation process in the form of purifying ritual.

Zeina's mandalas are special. So precise, and to me they vibrate with power. She finally started to share them on Instagram recently, during a time of deep grieving when she lost her mother to cancer.

The mandalas are all different. And even the repetition within the works are different. Some are dark and exude sadness; some are golden and vibrant, suggesting hope and creativity; another still is awash with colourful paints, calming and soft in its power. And they all begin in the centre, with a dot.

Zeina says making these mandalas is a way for her to be still, even though it's an activity that requires action. 'And just to do something for me,' she explains. 'Over the years I kept doing it. But I never validated what I was doing. It was almost like a secret because it was for me, it was for nobody else.'

Perhaps her most personal mandalas were for her mother, when she was critically ill with cancer. Zeina recounts with emotion how she created a healing mandala in the hope of easing her mother's pain. 'I never got a chance to finish it. But it was just [like asking]: what is healing? I just said, please universe, God almighty, let me make something that orbs into my mum; an essence, a healing energy . . .'

Zeina also created mandalas that only had on them 'la illaha il'Allah' (There is no God but God), the first part of the Islamic declaration of faith, and what is ideally a Muslim's final words.

The mandalas, she says, were filled with intention for her mother's wellbeing and comfort. And that is the essence of a mandala. A spiritual tool for healing and connection. Zeina shuffles the oracle deck one more time. She closes her eyes and selects her card. It's Wassily Kandinsky again, he of transcending systems to find spirit. She seems pleased as she reads the work advice: 'Hear music through sight.' But then comes the inspiration: 'Begin with a dot,' it suggests, and she shakes her head in wonder.

~~~~~

Of course, you don't need to make a living from, or have a consuming passion for, a creative pursuit to achieve catharsis. As the recent, if fading, trend in adult colouring books shows, stress relief can come through easier methods.

I am, however, a believer that creativity is our saviour. It is the thing that changes people, sparks us up, delivers relief and allows us to explore possibility. I have run creativity workshops at schools with kids bursting with creative potential. It's not unusual for emotions to run high, for these kids to come up to me and tell me about what they'd love to do but don't think they can. Often these are pursuits we generally see as creative: write, draw, act and so on.

But creativity can go further and deeper than producing work for others to consume. It does not have to be just one thing (I write; now I perform, too). You can be a lover of jewellery and make your own, and this is your own personal therapy kit. You might, like so many, find stillness and comfort in knitting. Even fitness, to me, can be creative, because the person doing the thing is creating an outcome. It's an expression of sorts. My former group training instructor, Joe, is athletic, but I consider him wildly creative for the consistent inventiveness of his sessions.

There is a reason why so many stories revolve around creative expression: it is a genuine pathway to liberation. It is a use of your mind and body in ways that can fulfil them. So, if you have not already, may I urge you to go forth and seek out your creative outlet? Once you find one, or even a few, and start practising, it will change your life. Do it consistently and you can't help but evolve and transform, and you will see the healing effects: more clarity, more purpose, and stronger relationships — including the one you have with yourself.

— CHAPTER EIGHT —

A Spiritual Path

From the outside, the centre for Sufi meditation looks like an ordinary house. The inside resembles a small mosque; at the entrance, wooden shelves are stuffed with shoes (they have to be removed), and Persian rugs blanket the floor. But instead of segregated prayer spaces or people seated in rows, worshippers sit against the walls, leaning into cushions, wrapped in blankets, as a recording plays.

I'm here for a Sufi meditation at the invitation of a friend. It's a welcoming space, to be sure. You don't have to be a Sufi to come along, though later, those of us who are visiting will break off from the Sufi meditators. The rooms will darken, and we will take a seat in the adjoining room near the entrance.

But first, people slowly filter in and find a spot some-where in the room. An overseer walks around, tray in hand, offering tea and sweets to the gathered.

I am respectful but feel strange being here, and find it hard to descend into a sense of quiet and reflection. I think it's primarily because the recitations playing out over the speaker are not in English; it's all in Farsi. Still, I have a sense of the emotion in the space, even if I have no comprehension of its poetry.

Beside me, a woman awakens from the recitations with wet eyes. It's been a while, she tells me. 'The truth is the hardest thing to find.'

I'm so touched by her manner, the sincerity in her being at that very moment. It crystallises for me that longing that propels so many of us. An innate but indefinable desire to connect to something greater than ourselves and, from that, find some extraordinary idea of love, and peace.

In his book 50 *Spiritual Classics*, another in the '50 Classics' series, Tom Butler-Bowdon follows on from his summary of self-help books that guide us on personal development. As touched on earlier, there is a great deal of crossover in MBS. One person's pragmatic self-help can easily overlap with another's New Age journey. It's easy to see why the field can get murky and increasingly difficult to define.

Butler-Bowdon's book on spiritual classics addresses the idea that humans are not ultimately satisfied by material quests, security or vast knowledge: 'we were built to seek answers to larger questions'.

The Online Etymology Dictionary notes that 'spiritual' is derived directly from 'a Medieval Latin ecclesiastical use of Latin *spiritualis* "of or pertaining to breath, breathing, wind, or air; pertaining to spirit", from *spiritus* "of breathing, of the spirit".'

Butler-Bowdon takes note: breathing is something we all do. Spiritual experience, he says, 'is what makes us human'.

Spiritual pursuit, to my mind, involves a letting go in order to find truth, and a connection to something greater than ourselves.

This idea takes on more clarity when, a few days after I meet with her, The Modern Witch Stacey Demarco sends me a note. She's been thinking about our conversation on witchcraft and paganism. She'd spent an afternoon in a local national park, trekking to a high point, where she stopped to take in the view and have a snack.

'I noticed how much trash was over one side of the area. The idea that people would bother to walk into this place (and a two-hour hike is the only way), enjoy nature and then leave their rubbish, is in a way the ultimate in disconnection.'

Stacey pulled out a garbage bag and cleaned it up, leaving with the rubbish. Her hike in nature was an homage to the goddess Artemis, she who is wild and free, but better still, Stacey says, an opportunity to clean up her domain. 'Protection of these places is vital,' she writes. 'There is a lot of spiritual fashion right now around "women's wildness" and it expresses itself with lots of flower crowns, boho fashion, selfies and crystal mandalas under a full moon,' Stacey continues. 'How many of these "wild women" actually step into the wild? How many go solo into the quiet places of green, or sleep upon the earth away from the lights and selfies? Or run with their hounds or ride in union with a horse? How many actually find themselves in a natural place and have the opportunity to clean it?'

They are valuable questions to ask. I wonder, then, if we have lost the point altogether of what it means to be at one with the world we inhabit?

For Stacey, living with a 'wild mentor' like Artemis (one of the oldest of the animist deities) leads you to genuine action, and to 'forget the faux'. 'We begin to find again the wildness we all have tucked away in our muscles, our pulsing blood and heart and of course in our feet, and we begin to live authentically again,' she tells me.

I think about her words a lot in the days to come. The cult of commodifying spirituality. Or what Caroline Myss calls 'spiritual depression' (which is akin to a 'dark night of the soul', a crisis of spirituality rather than mental health), and Colette Baron-Reid calls 'spiritual narcolepsy'. 'We fall asleep once in a while and let fear take the wheel,' Colette writes in *Uncharted*.

Neither is very good — the faux or the fear.

The words 'live authentically again' linger the most in my mind. It so simply encapsulates what I am trying to distil in this exploration of all things New Age. We begin with a tool or a practice, a set of ideas and beliefs. Ideally, we evolve from those things, but not towards acquiring more stuff, or deepening ideas and experiences for their own sake, so that we never have to really live with ourselves. Striving all of the time isn't the point — surely an authentic life is one that is more effortless.

GOING BEYOND THOUGHT

Angela Lyos Braun is a Vedic meditation teacher who studied under Thom Knoles, a master-teacher (known as a *maharishi*). Vedic meditation is a transcending meditation brought to the West (and to The Beatles) by Maharishi Mahesh Yogi decades ago.

At dinner one night, as I am in the thick of researching this book, she tells me that Joseph Campbell was a student of Vedic knowledge and I mention that he seems to tap into this idea of 'oneness'. This is akin to the 'universal consciousness' of the New Age, and Carl Jung's 'collective unconscious'.

'You are consciousness. I am consciousness. You are that. I am that. All this is nothing but that,' says Angela. 'This is the basic fundamental teachings of the Veda. You are consciousness, you are Bliss . . .'

Bliss. In Vedic meditation, there comes a point where you transcend; it's so blissful that the mind falls mute. You are in Being, in pure consciousness, pure awareness. 'Bliss,' says Angela with emphasis. 'Not bliss as in ecstasy, like in those photos where you see everyone with their hands up. Bliss as in a supreme inner contentedness where nothing else matters. You don't know that you're there. You just know, when you come out of there, that something beautiful has happened.'

While religion can sometimes lead people to feel unworthy, Vedic knowledge says you deserve the best. Happiness does not need to be found, but uncovered.

I tell Angela that so many people are looking for happiness like it's a magic pill. Doing things that offer moments of relief, finding a peace that can't be sustained once the real world sneaks back in.

'The Vedic world view — a body of knowledge that precedes all religions, all philosophies — tells us that we are happiness. So happiness is you, but you need to uncover that.'

But, beyond the 'hard matter' — the stuff we can touch, see and feel — what are we? Angela starts to speak in scientific terms, ideas that could make up a book of their own, so I won't try to simplify them. But the ultimate point of her discussion of cells, atoms, molecules and particles is to demonstrate that smaller particles, called 'lepto quarks' or 'leptons', appear as 'waves' under a high-speed camera. 'They rise and collapse. Activity, non-activity.'

This science is relevant to Vedic meditation because, as a transcending technique, this is what we are doing all the time — imitating nature. We go from activity (life) into silence (meditation); from our individuality then back into universality (oneness). We, too, are waves, rising and collapsing. Waves collapsing back into the ocean, to oneness.

'When we meditate, we're getting to the subtlest strata of the mind and beyond, to "the source of thought".'

All roads lead to meditation. It's the one practice that comes in enough different forms that even the most hardened critic of New Age modalities might find some respite.

But Vedic meditation differs from other types of meditation: practices that focus on concentration techniques; guided meditations, where you journey to other realms; meditations that promote contemplation techniques or gratitude; and more.

'Everything works, to some degree,' says Angela. 'But those practices keep the mind on the active layer, or just below the active layer, because you're thinking about something. In Vedic meditation, what happens is that you go beyond thinking . . . it's a transcending technique. So you're transcending all those thoughts and moving to the subtle strata of the mind where there's hardly any thought. And then eventually you step beyond to this place of no thoughts, of just Being.'

Vedic meditation employs a mantra, different for each person, and meant to be kept private. It's a mellifluous-sounding word; it's a vibration, and meaningless; a mind vehicle designed to deliver you to those subtle states, not to be mistaken for a mantra meditation that requires recitation.

Angela says the practice is to 'go within' twice a day for twenty minutes each session. The repetition of the practice sees this blissful state embed slowly until our baseline is Bliss.

Angela's enthusiasm is evident, and contagious. 'Scientists have done research on this.' See *The Neurophysiology of Enlightenment* by Dr Robert Keith Wallace, Angela says. 'After a few years, they found [the subjects] had a completely different physiological signature. Different brainwave patterns, heart rate, blood pressure.'

I ask Angela what this experience of Bliss looks like in the real world.

'Where other people are getting stressed and staying stressed, you're not staying stressed. There's nothing wrong with getting stressed, stress can save your life . . . you step in front of traffic, a car beeps its horn, you immediately step back. It's a survival response. Staying stressed is the problem.'

Angela offers an example of the sort of problem a person might experience. 'People say, "I was broken-hearted, and I stayed broken-hearted for years." This stuff doesn't happen when you have this baseline of Bliss, because you know that you are not your thoughts. You are not all this other stuff: where I grew up and all these things that happened to me during my childhood.'

While a lot of New Age practice is powered by promises of unleashing potential, of becoming special or almost superhuman, Angela's offering is less shiny, though — for me — more enticing. You will intuit better, she says, and you will also 'follow charm', which is to say, you will more easily go in the direction of something that appeals to you, or do things that just feel right or necessary without unpacking why. The mind, too, wants to follow charm, she adds, and move towards evolution. 'Everything is always evolving,' Angela says. 'We move in the direction of relevance.'

The more you meditate, the more you clear out the mental clutter, the better you are able to detect charm. The going within twice a day also leads to a sharpening of our senses.

'When your intuition is heightened, then you know, as a meditator, which direction to take. You see the signs. You're following charm.'

The mantra stands out among all the chatter of the mind. 'We think it ever so effortlessly,' says Angela. It is a 'vibration', and the nature of vibration is akin to plucking a guitar string.

'It'll be loud in the beginning, but then it gets softer, vaguer, finer, fainter. The mind finds that very charming, and it follows it. This gets softer and vaguer and infinitesimally faint, and the mind follows it, and eventually it steps beyond, because you're right at the end of the spectrum, you're at the source of thought. Most charming.'

It doesn't take any convincing to get me to try it. I just know, in some strange way, that this is another answer to my spiritual confusion and malaise.

Angela strikes me as a good ambassador for what she teaches. She talks about being in the world with more elegance and sophistication, and this is how I have always seen her. A calm, measured spirit in a turbulent world.

I sign up to learn. In a private *puja* ceremony, Angela gives thanks to her teachers, and blesses offerings of fruit and flowers. Afterwards, she gives me my mantra, instructing me on how to effortlessly play it in my mind. For four mornings we meet, we practise the meditation, and she talks about what to expect. Un-stressing, she advises, is part of the process. In other words, releasing long-held emotions and the like. She says that it might feel like I'm not succeeding, especially if I start to overflow with emotion.

'There are times when the meditation is a bit more turbulent than others. It takes a while to liberate stresses from the past . . . a lot of thoughts and memories come up, but they go very quickly . . . The results are immediate and cumulative. So the more you meditate, the easier it becomes. So now when things come your way, they really just wash off.'

In a sublime piece for the *Quarterly Essay*, art critic Sebastian Smee considers the inner life and its corruption in a modern world drenched in technology and distractions.

He tries to define it, acknowledging that your inner life 'may be obscure, even to yourself'. The obscurity is a worry at a time when social media captures so much of our attention. A friend of his says that we're all basically algorithms. Smee acknowledges some truth to this, but also admits to his own sentimentality about how he sees the world: he doesn't feel like an algorithm.

Because Smee is concerned with the presence of a digital life, he talks about how we are trained now to overshare our lives.

This seeking of approval or acceptance is heavy in the New Age world. It's also set up for showmanship because there is an obsession with proof from the outside world.

On this need to impress with our spiritual ascension and success, I turn back to Smee, who so articulately sums up why it bothers me, the way it carves into the authentic richness of a moment. We may feel the need to connect to others for the sake of sanity, but these social media shares can betray 'the primary, inward experience'. Soon, Smee grows even more poetic in his exploration of the inner life: 'It is not some placid lake in a forest. It is tumultuous, provisional, unsettling.'

Smee's essay affected me profoundly. It's not that he instructed me in how to think. Rather, he so eloquently put into words how I feel.

I was similarly moved when Joseph Campbell, in *The Power of Myth*, characterised the soul's journey in similar terms: 'The inner world is the world of your requirements and your energies and your structure and your possibilities that meets the outer world. And the outer world is the field of your incarnation. That's where you are. You've got to keep both going.'

Our inner life is connected to our outer one; they reflect each other. But increasingly, the external world and the solutions within it demand too much of us. And this is where the danger lies — missing the point of a spiritual practice, which, hopefully, is more than an indulgence. Rather, it's about a peaceful inner and outer life; it's about getting to a place of being where you are able to exist in the world without unnecessary fear; where your contentment is not reliant on how others live and perceive you. And for the lucky seekers, it's about a life infused with divinity in some form. It's about oneness and surrender. Grounded, but in many ways, unreal.

CONCLUSION

At the start of this book, I pondered why we need so many ways to feel better, to connect to God or other divine forces, and what we expect to find when we do. What do we want? To know ourselves or God? I think, in a way, both. After all, even the more vocal anti-woo types spend a great deal of time countering other people's beliefs. Most of us, I would say, are seeking ways to express ourselves, and for many it's through devotion.

In a more socially and technologically connected world, how we manage these approaches has shifted. In an idle few moments before a gym class, this crystallised for me. My friend in the Arab world, Nikita, who has healed trauma through conscious dance and yoga, was posting about a new book called *McMindfulness: How Mindfulness Became the New Capitalist Spirituality* by Ronald E. Purser. Like me, she sees the holes in the ever-expanding universe of the New Age and MBS, but also like me, has experienced firsthand the profound benefits of living a more rounded life, of dissolving into a spiritual moment.

It occurred to me how, for a long time, different sides of myself have been fighting each other: the one that loves the mystery, the one that relies on logic and analysis, and the one that drowns in self-consciousness.

As I worked on this book, I wound my way through my heritage, a storied Arabian history revealed, one that encompasses magic and mystery in spades. I saw how this history influences and relates to what now exists in the world, but also how deeply it sits within me, a rich inheritance. For most of my life, I have tried to make sense of existence through a spiritual lens. The beating heart of it all has always been connection in various forms — to God, to mystery, to others, to myself, to a thread of purpose. And perhaps now I understand better that it's not a lens I need, but a way of being.

So this book isn't simply an exploratory confessional or a guide — it's a love letter to the world in which I was raised, and the ever-expanding one I carefully curate, one filled with questions, yes, but also possibility and joy in the not-knowing.

What I do know is that there is no quick fix. And you don't need to empty your wallet to find bliss. But it requires some investment and effort, this journey of getting to know yourself better. Your inner and outer worlds are inextricably linked, but how that plays out for each of us will be different. It takes some experimentation and a willingness to be amazed or disappointed to find practices that improve your life, and how you deal with the hard stuff.

No single route is a no-brainer for everyone, just because it is for you, or for me. I wrote this book not simply to make sense of this for myself, but for you, the reader, the seeker who knows they want something more fulfilling, or who has an inkling that there might be something to all this. Yes, surely, no matter your limits when it comes to the wonderful world of woo woo, there is something to all of this.

ACKNOWLEDGEMENTS

Just as I was finishing the final major edit on this book, I was visiting my massage therapist, Karen, who, suggested that I approach a woman who does Human Design: a mash-up of existing modalities that takes a grounded approach to your personality type and how you best thrive. The mini-report is free, as is a half-hour consultation. Of course, I did it.

The woman, Barbara, told me that I am a 'generator' (a 'get things done' type), and that I respond best to opportunity based on gut instinct (ha!). She also assigned me numbers that explained other aspects of my personality (which I won't go into here). But what struck me the most was when she told me to think of a maps app, which gives you the best route to take to your destination, but also recommends alternative ones. 'That's you,' she said. I do the work to see all the different routes then share it for others' benefit. She had no idea I had just spent two years trying to do exactly that with this book, and it was a reassuring observation. And really, when my work on this book began, I had unknowingly been researching this world for years.

I start my acknowledgements with this story because this book has been one of my most difficult creative endeavours. All writers will tell you that every project carves out little pieces of you, and you never feel the same. It can be creatively fulfilling, but after writing *Cleo* (which became my nickname for the book), I felt like I had been put through a tumble dryer on repeat.

I have emerged clearer but the period of disorientation was deep and long: I was the maps app trying to figure out how to share multiple routes, to work out if they were viable or relevant, even when one seemed easier than the rest.

When the book looked like it was going to sputter and completely die following over a year of work, a timely connection with my publisher, Kelly Doust, revived it. Thank you, Kelly, for your swift and complete embrace of this book and your faith in me. You are a special soul and I find you completely inspiring and wonderful.

Thank you to the rest of the Murdoch Books team who helped get this book into shape. First, Roberta Ivers, who had the unenviable task of leading the structural edit. I had a feeling when I first met you at a writers festival a couple of years ago that we would work together one day, though I wasn't to know it would involve wrangling two drafts of a monster book.

Rebecca Hamilton, your job was as challenging, and your patience and sensitivity throughout the copyedit meant more to me than I can say. Thank you for your care and enthusiasm.

Thank you also to Julie Mazur Tribe for being a gentle and warm leader in this process, and for allowing this project the space and time it needed.

As always, I give thanks to my agent, Tara Wynne at Curtis Brown, who patiently helped me work out how to pitch a book about the New Age and spirituality that is 'kind of a memoir but not really'. Your insight is eternally appreciated. And thank you to the rest of Curtis Brown team for your ongoing support.

Deepest gratitude to my family, who I have been on this spiritual journey with from the start — especially my mother, an insightful explorer from whom I think I also get my scepticism, and my father, who consistently tells me that I can be the next Colleen McCullough.

An extra special thanks to my husband, Chris Larsen, who didn't blink when I told him that I was thinking about travelling to Phoenix, Arizona, to attend a conference called Celebrate Your Life! — you are my rock.

To my close girlfriends, many of whom I have known since childhood — you have always been so beautifully supportive of me and my work. I love you guys.

I thank all of my interviewees, who opened their hearts and minds to me as I tried to unpack the world of the seeker. I have to give a special nod to Colette Baron-Reid — our meeting and connection was a true moment of synchronicity I treasure. Who knew when I bought my first Colette Baron-Reid oracle deck that one day we'd be friends?

There are many people I have worked with or encountered over the years who have made a difference in my life. I want to offer particular thanks to Denise Jarvie, Patty Kikos, Stacey Demarco, Catalina Corrales, Karen Riley, Angela Lyos Braun, Jasmine Hawkins and Claire Hickson. You are genuine healers and I am so lucky to know you.

ACKNOWLEDGEMENTS

There are so many people I am grateful to because in some way, big or small, they have contributed to this journey through connection or participation. I am sorry I don't have the capacity to thank you all individually, but I am sending you big loving vibes always.

ACKNOWLEDGEMENTS

NOTES

Introduction

Cooper, D., *Atlantis Cards,* Great Britain: Findhorn Press Ltd, 2005

Pearce, S., *The Alchemy of Voice*, Great Britain: Findhorn Press Ltd, 2010

Pearce, S., *Angels of Atlantis*, Great Britain: Findhorn Press Ltd, 2011

Greenwood, S., *The Encyclopedia of Magic & Witchcraft*, Leicestershire: Anness Publishing Ltd 2001

The Encyclopedia of Crystals, Herbs, & New Age Elements, US: Simon & Schuster, 2016

Butler-Bowdon, T., *50 Self-Help Classics*, Great Britain: John Murray Press, 2017

Chapter One

Redfield, J., *The Celestine Prophecy*, Australia: Transworld Publishers (Division of Random House Australia), 2011

Walsch, N.D., *Conversations with God*, Great Britain: Hodder & Stoughton, 1997

Dispenza, Dr J., *Breaking the Habit of Being Yourself*, US: Hay House Inc, 2012

Williamson, M., *A Return to Love*, Great Britain: HarperCollins Publishers, 1997

Schucman, H., *A Course in Miracles*, US: Foundation for Inner Peace; 3rd edn, 2008

Myss, C., *Sacred Contracts*, US: Bantam Doubleday Dell
  Publishing Group Inc, 2002

Cody, N., 'Is this life of mine my fault?', *Cauldrons and Cupcakes*
  by Nicole Cody, 2017, <www.cauldronsandcupcakes.
  com/2017/08/31/is-this-life-of-mine-my-fault>

Andersen, K., 'Oprah Winfrey Helped Create Our American
  Fantasyland', *Slate*, 2018, <www.slate.com/health-and-
  science/2018/01/oprah-winfrey-helped-create-our-irrational-
  pseudoscientific-american-fantasyland.html>

Featherstone, E., 'Crystals, potions and tarot cards: the mystical
  rise of new age businesses', *The Guardian*, 2018, <www.the
  guardian.com/small-business-network/2018/jan/18/crystals-
  potions-and-tarot-cards-the-mystical-rise-of-new-age-businesses>

Bichard, T., 'Artists turn to tarot to ask what the future holds',
  Dazed, 2017, <www.dazeddigital.com/artsandculture/article/
  34149/1/artists-turn-to-tarot-to-ask-what-the-future-holds>

Sullivan, A., 'America's New Religions', Intelligencer, *New York*
  magazine, 2018, <www.nymag.com/intelligencer/2018/12/
  andrew-sullivan-americas-new-religions.html>

De Botton, A., *Religion for Atheists*, Great Britain: Penguin Books
  Ltd, 2014

Sagan, S., *For Small Creatures Such as We*, Australia: Murdoch
  Books, 2019

Watterson, M., *The Divine Feminine Oracle,* US: Hay House Inc,
  2018

Delaney, B., *Wellmania*, Australia: Black Inc, 2017

Kondo, M., *The Life-Changing Magic of Tidying Up*, US: Ten
  Speed Press, 2014

Dilloway, M., 'What White, Western Audiences Don't
  Understand About Marie Kondo's "Tidying Up"', *HuffPost*,
  2019, <huffpost.com/entry/marie-kondo-white-western-
  audineces_n_5c47859be4b025aa26bde77c>

Schofield, A., 'What we gain from keeping books — and why it
  doesn't need to be "joy"', *The Guardian*, 2019, <www.the
  guardian.com/books/2019/jan/07/what-we-gain-from-keeping-
  books-and-why-it-doesnt-need-to-be-joy-marie-kondo>

NOTES

Cromb, N., '"Appreciation", "spiritual connection" . . . Nope, you are not entitled to appropriate our culture', NITV, 2017, <www.sbs.com.au/nitv/article/2017/10/20/appreciation-spiritual-connection-nope-you-are-not-entitled-appropriate-our-1>

Baron-Reid, C., *Goddess Power Oracle*, US: Hay House Inc, 2019

Baron-Reid, C., *Wisdom of the Hidden Realms*, US: Hay House Inc, 2010

Baron-Reid, C., *Wisdom of the Oracle*, US: Hay House Inc, 2015

'I Was So High', This American Life, Episode 524, 2 May 2014, <www.thisamericanlife.org/524/i-was-so-high>

Weinberg, S., *Crystals and the New Age*, US: Ibis Press, 2012

Dunbar-Ortiz, R., 'White Americans need to stop assuming Native American culture belongs to them, too', *Quartz*, 2016, <www.qz.com/805704/columbus-day-cultural-appropriation-white-americans-need-to-stop-assuming-native-american-culture-belongs-to-them-too>

York, M., 'New Age Commodification and Appropriation of Spirituality' (Abstract), Journal of Contemporary Religion, 2010, <www.tandfonline.com/doi/abs/10.1080/13537900120077177>

Watts, A., *Just So: An Odyssey into the Cosmic Web of Connection, Play, and True Pleasure* (audio recording): Sounds True, 2017

Thornely, J., *Zealot: A Book about Cults*, Australia: Hachette, 2019

Campbell, J. with Moyers, B., *The Power of Myth*, US: Bantam Doubleday Dell Publishing Group Inc, 1991

Virtue, D., 'An A–Z List of New Age Practices to Avoid, and Why', *Doreen Virtue*, 2019, <www.doreenvirtue.com/2019/07/21/an-a-z-list-of-new-age-practices-to-avoid-and-why>

Chapter Two
Gronlund, M., 'It's now an emoji, but what's the story of the evil eye amulet?', *The National*, 2018, <www.thenational.ae/arts-culture/art/it-s-now-an-emoji-but-what-s-the-story-of-the-evil-eye-amulet-1.798929>

El-Zein, A., *Islam, Arabs, and the Intelligent World of the Jinn*, US: Syracuse University Press, 2017

Ruiz, D.M. & Emrys, B., *The Three Questions*, Great Britain: HarperCollins Publishers, 2018

Greenwood, S., *The Encyclopedia of Magic & Witchcraft*, Leicestershire: Anness Publishing Ltd 2001

Campbell, J. with Moyers, B., *The Power of Myth*, US: Bantam Doubleday Dell Publishing Group Inc, 1991

Chapter Three

Hay, L., *You Can Heal Your Life — 30th Anniversary Edition*, US: Hay House Inc, 2017

Awad, A., 'Growing Pains', *ELLE magazine*, 2013

Hendricks, G., *The Big Leap*, US: HarperCollins Publishers, 2010

Ruiz, D.M., *The Mastery of Love*, US: Amber-Allen Publishing, 1999

Ruiz, D.M., *The Four Agreements*, US: Amber-Allen Publishing, 2011

Ruiz, D.M. & Mills, J., *The Fifth Agreement*, US: Amber-Allen Publishing, 2012

Manson, M., *The Subtle Art of Not Giving a F*ck*, Australia: Pan Macmillan Australia, 2016

Knight, S., *The Life-Changing Magic of Not Giving a F*ck*, US: Little, Brown & Company, 2015

Economakis, F., *Harden the F*ck Up*, Australia: New Holland Publishers, 2017

Bennett, Dr M. & Bennett, S., *F*ck Feelings*, Great Britain: HarperCollins Publishers, 2016

Parkin, J.C., *F*ck It: Be At Peace With Life Just As It Is*, Great Britain: Hay House Inc, 2018

Owen, A., *How to Stop Feeling Like Sh*t*, Australia: Black Inc, 2018

Duffield-Thomas, D., *Get Rich, Lucky B*tch!*, Great Britain: Hay House UK, 2018

Bishop, G.J., *Unf*ck Yourself*, Great Britain: Hodder & Stoughton, 2017

NOTES

Hay, L., *You Can Heal Your Life — 30th Anniversary Edition*, US: Hay House Inc, 2017

Carnegie, D., *How to Win Friends and Influence People*, Australia: HarperCollins Publishers, 2017

Butler-Bowdon, T., *50 Self-Help Classics*, Great Britain: John Murray Press, 2017

Brown, B., *Daring Greatly*, Great Britain: Penguin Books Ltd, 2016

Robbins, A., *Awaken the Giant Within*, US: Simon & Schuster, 2001

Chopra, D., *The Seven Spiritual Laws of Success*, US: Amber-Allen Publishing, 1995

Campbell, J. with Moyers, B., *The Power of Myth*, US: Bantam Doubleday Dell Publishing Group Inc, 1991

Coelho, P., *The Alchemist*, US: HarperCollins Publishers, 2006

Jeffers, S., *Feel the Fear and Do It Anyway*, Great Britain: Ebury Publishing, 2007

Covey, S., *The Seven Habits of Highly Successful People — 25th Anniversary Edition*, US: Simon & Schuster, 2013

Gray, J., *Men are from Mars, Women are from Venus — Special Edition*, Great Britain: HarperCollins Publishers, 2012

Cederström, C., *The Happiness Fantasy*, Great Britain: Polity Press, 2018

Grieve, C., 'LEGO, Super Mario and pimple cream best-sellers for Amazon's first year in Australia', *Sydney Morning Herald*, 2018, <www.smh.com.au/business/companies/lego-super-mario-and-pimple-cream-best-sellers-for-amazon-s-first-year-in-australia-20181204-p50k6q.html>

Hicks, E. & J., *The Vortex*, US: Hay House Inc, 2019

Hay, L., *You Can Heal Your Life — 30th Anniversary Edition*, US: Hay House Inc, 2017

Hay, L., *Heal Your Body*, US: Hay House Inc, 1984

Nelson, Dr B., *The Emotion Code*, Great Britain; Ebury Publishing, 2019

Carnegie, D., *How to Win Friends and Influence People*, Australia: HarperCollins Publishers, 2017

Hay, L., *You Can Heal Your Life — 30th Anniversary Edition*, US: Hay House Inc, 2017

NOTES

Tolle, E., *The Power of Now*, Australia: Hachette Australia, 2011

His Holiness the Dalai Lama & Cutler, H.C., *The Art of Happiness: A Handbook for Living*, Australia: Hachette Australia, 1998

Byrne, R., *The Secret — The 10th Anniversary Edition*, US: Atria Books, 2006

Robbins, A., *Awaken the Giant Within*, US: Simon & Schuster, 2001

Covey, S., *The Seven Habits of Highly Successful People — 25th Anniversary Edition*, US: Simon & Schuster, 2013

Miguel Ruiz, D., *The Mastery of Love*, US: Amber-Allen Publishing, 1999

Murphy, J., *The Power of Your Subconscious Mind*, US: Prentice Hall Press, 2011

Chopra, D., *Quantum Healing*, US: Random House USA Inc, 2015

Jeffers, S., *Feel the Fear and Do It Anyway*, Great Britain: Ebury Publishing, 2007

Hicks, E. & J., *The Vortex*, US: Hay House Inc, 2019

Dispenza, Dr J., *Breaking the Habit of Being Yourself*, US: Hay House Inc, 2012

Manson, M., *The Subtle Art of Not Giving a F*ck*, Australia: Pan Macmillan Australia, 2016

Manson, M., *Everything is F*cked: A Book about Hope*, US: HarperCollins Publishers, 2019

Knight, S., *The Life-Changing Magic of Not Giving a F*ck*, US: Little, Brown & Company, 2015

Kondo, M., *The Life-Changing Magic of Tidying Up*, US: Ten Speed Press, 2014

Chapter Four

Novella, S. with Novella, B., Santa Maria, C., Novella, J. & Bernstein, E., *The Skeptics' Guide to the Universe*, Great Britain: Hodder & Stoughton, 2019

D'Entremont, Y., 'The "Food Babe" Blogger Is Full of Shit', *Gawker*, 2015, <gawker.com/the-food-babe-blogger-is-full-of-shit-1694902226>

Gunter, Dr J., 'Dear Gwyneth Paltrow, I'm a GYN and your vaginal jade eggs are a bad idea', 2017, <drjengunter.

com/2017/01/17/dear-gwyneth-paltrow-im-a-gyn-and-your-
vaginal-jade-eggs-are-a-bad-idea>

Davey, M., 'Jessica Ainscough, Australia's "wellness warrior",
dies of cancer aged 30', *The Guardian*, 1 March 2015,
<www.theguardian.com/australia-news/2015/mar/01/jessica-
ainscough-australia-wellness-warrior-dies-cancer-aged-30>

Douglas, J., 'Behind Belle Gibson's cancer con: "Everything
about this story is extreme"', *The Guardian,* 13 November
2017, <www.theguardian.com/books/2017/nov/13/
behind-belle-gibsons-cancer-con-everything-about-this-story-
is-extreme>

Chapter Five

IBISWorld, 'Psychic Services Industry in the US — Market
Research Report', 2019, <www.ibisworld.com/united-states/
market-research-reports/psychic-services-industry/>

Gecewicz, C., '"New Age" beliefs common among both religious
and nonreligious Americans', Pew Research Center, 2018,
<www.pewresearch.org/fact-tank/2018/10/01/new-age-beliefs-
common-among-both-religious-and-nonreligious-americans>

Baron-Reid, C., *The Spirit Animal Oracle*, US: Hay House Inc,
2018

Baron-Reid, C., *Wisdom of the Oracle*, US: Hay House Inc, 2015

Baron-Reid, C., *The Good Tarot,* US: Hay House Inc, 2017

Baron-Reid, C., *The Enchanted Map*, US: Hay House Inc, 2011

Baron-Reid, C., *The Crystal Spirits Oracle*, US: Hay House Inc,
2019

Weigel, J., *Psychics, Healers & Mediums*, US: Hampton Roads
Publishing, 2017

Holland J., *The Psychic Tarot*, US: Hay House Inc, 2009

Holland J., *The Psychic Tarot for the Heart*, US: Hay House Inc,
2014

Holland J. and Pearlman, C., *Born Knowing*, US: Hay House Inc,
2003

Crossing Over with John Edward (TV show), US: Sci-Fi Channel,
2001

Waite, A. E., *The Rider-Waite Tarot Deck*, US: U.S. Games Systems Inc, 2015

Crowley, A., *The Thoth Tarot*, US: US Games Systems Inc, 2000

Hall, A., *Simply Tarot*, Australia: Hinkler Books Pty Ltd, 2005

Road, C. C., *Next World Tarot,* US: Silver Sprocket, 2019

Fairchild, A., *The White Light Oracle*, Australia: Blue Angel Publishing, 2019

Fairchild, A., *Crystal Stars 11.11*, Australia: Blue Angel Publishing, 2019

Harnish, C. L., *Return of Spirit*, US: Spirit's Way Designs, 2018

Eno B. and Schmidt, P., *Oblique Strategies* (5th edition), UK: 2001

Meiklejohn-Free, B. and Peters, F. K., *Divination of the Ancients*, Australia: Blue Angel Publishing, 2016

Chapter Six

The One (TV show), Australia: Seven Network, 2008

Cunningham, S., *Earth, Air, Fire & Water*, US: Llewellyn Publications, 2002

Greenwood, S., *The Encyclopedia of Magic & Witchcraft*, Leicestershire: Anness Publishing Ltd 2001

RavenWolf, S., *To Light a Sacred Flame*, US: Llewellyn Publications US, 2002

Cavendish, L., *Witches and Wizards,* The Supernatural Series Book One, Australia: Rockpool Publishing, 2016

Dell, C., *The Occult, Witchcraft & Magic*, UK: Thames & Hudson Ltd, 2016

Crofts, C., 'The Witch of Kings Cross', *National Geographic*, 2016, <www.nationalgeographic.com.au/history/the-witch-of-kings-cross.aspx>

Wappler, M., 'Jenna Dewan's New Dawn', *Harper's Bazaar*, 2018, <www.harpersbazaar.com/culture/features/a20876029/jenna-dewan-interview>

Gaiman, N., *Norse Mythology*, Great Britain: Bloomsbury Publishing, 2018

Miller, M., *Circe*, Great Britain: Bloomsbury Publishing, 2019

Tóibín, C., *House of Names*, Great Britain: Penguin Books Ltd, 2018

NOTES

Fry, S., *Mythos*, Great Britain: Penguin Books Ltd, 2018

Von Worms, A., *The Book of Abramelin: A New Translation* (G. Dehn, ed., S. Guth, trans.), US: Ibis Press, 2015

Greenwood, S., *The Encyclopedia of Magic & Witchcraft*, Leicestershire: Anness Publishing Ltd 2001

Carroll, P. J., *Liber Null & Psychonaut: An Introduction to Chaos Magic*, US: Red Wheel/Weiser, 1987

Carroll, P. J., *Principia Chaotica*, <www.sacred-texts.com/eso/ chaos/princhao.txt>

Gilbert, E., *Big Magic*, Great Britain: Bloomsbury Publishing, 2016

Dispenza, Dr J., *Breaking the Habit of Being Yourself*, US: Hay House Inc, 2012

Dispenza, Dr J., *You Are The Placebo*, US: Hay House Inc, 2014

A Wrinkle in Time (film), US: Walt Disney Pictures and Whitaker Entertainment, 2018

BlackTree TV, interview by Lashay, J., 'A Wrinkle in Time in depth interviews (Oprah, Reese, Mindy, Ava, Storm, Gugu and Chris)', 2018, <https://www.youtube.com/ watch?v=bsGCz0Sh4-0>

Dispenza, Dr J., *Becoming Supernatural*, US: Hay House Inc, 2017

Awad, A., 'The fascination with divination', *SBS Life*, 2016, <www.sbs.com.au/topics/voices/culture/article/2016/06/08/ fascination-divination>

The Princess Bride (film), US: Act III Communications, Buttercup Films Ltd and The Princess Bride Ltd, 1987

Fairchild, A., *Sacred Rebels Oracle*, Australia: Blue Angel Publishing, 2014

Hendricks, G., *The Joy of Genius*, US: Waterside Publishing, 2018

Chapter Seven

Weinberg, S., *Crystals and the New Age*, US: Ibis Press, 2012

Awad, A., *Courting Samira*, Australia: Self-published, 2011

Awad, A., 'All shook up' — Writers' piece, *frankie*, Issue 87, Jan/Feb 2019

Gilbert, E., *Big Magic*, Great Britain: Bloomsbury Publishing, 2016

NOTES

Tylevich, K. & Sommer, M., *Art Oracles*, Great Britain: Laurence King, 2017

Chapter Eight
Butler-Bowdon, T., *50 Spiritual Classics*, Great Britain: John Murray Press, 2017
Origin of 'spiritual', Online Etymology Dictionary, <www.etymonline.com/word/spiritual>
Baron-Reid, C., *Uncharted*, US: Hay House Inc, 2016
Swanson, G., *The Neurophysiology of Enlightenment*, US: Dharma Publications, 2016
Smee, S., 'Net Loss: The Inner Life in the Digital Age', *Quarterly Essay*, Issue 72, Australia: Black Inc, 2018
Campbell, J. with Moyers, B., *The Power of Myth*, US: Bantam Doubleday Dell Publishing Group Inc, 1991

Conclusion
Purser, R., *McMindfulness: How Mindfulness Became the New Capitalist Spirituality*, Great Britain: Watkins Media, 2019

NOTES

RESOURCES

For details of the publications mentioned in this book, please refer to the endnotes.

HELPFUL LINKS
Events and organisations
Australian Skeptics: www.skeptics.com.au

Celebrate Your Life!: www.celebrateyourlife.com

Mind Body Spirit Festival (Australia): www.mbsfestival.com.au

Meditation
Angela Lyos Braun — Vedic Meditation:
   www.angelalyosmeditation.com

Denise Jarvie — Living Meditation gatherings:
   www.denisejarvie.com

Headspace: www.headspace.com

Self-improvement
Aura-Soma: www.aura-soma.com

Natureluster: www.natureluster.com

Stin Hansen — My Thought Coach: www.mythoughtcoach.com

Crystals

Mineralism: www.mineralism.com.au

Dance

5Rhythms: www.5rhythms.com

IMOVE Foundation: www.imovefoundation.org

Jo Cobbett — Movinground: www.movinground.com

Esotericism and folklore

Ali A Olomi on Twitter (Historian of Middle East & Islam: Muslim politics, gender, Islamic esotericism and folklore; host of #HeadOnHistory Podcast): www.twitter.com/aaolomi

Mandala art

Zeina Iaali on Instagram: @zeina_iaali_artist

Reiki

Blended Insight: www.youtube.com/channel/UCeeKY7Vt_24Ku 3h_wH0azCA/featured

Divine White Light: www.youtube.com/channel/UCLlIF0DEBJc0oJZ4gLipPbg

RestRelaxationReiki: www.youtube.com/user/RestRelaxationReiki

Intuitive readings for the collective

Cheryl Lee Harnish: www.youtube.com/user/CherylLeeHarnish

Colette Baron-Reid: www.youtube.com/user/ColetteBaronReid

FURTHER SUPPORT

Note: many organisations for women are state-based and too numerous to list. Please undertake a local search for your nearest and most appropriate organisation.

The Arts Wellbeing Collective
Mental health for performing artists:
www.artswellbeingcollective.com.au

Beyond Blue
Anxiety, depression and suicide prevention:
www.beyondblue.org.au

Black Dog Institute
Mental health treatment: www.blackdoginstitute.org.au

Blue Knot Helpline
Childhood trauma: www.blueknot.org.au

Butterfly Foundation
Eating disorders: www.thebutterflyfoundation.org.au

Carers Australia
Carers: www.carersaustralia.com.au

Flourish Australia
*Mental health recovery and wellbeing for people with a lived
experience*: www.flourishaustralia.org.au

Gidget Foundation
Perinatal depression and anxiety: www.gidgetfoundation.org.au

Kids Helpline
Counselling for ages 5–25: www.kidshelpline.com.au

Lifeline
Crisis support and suicide prevention: www.lifeline.org.au

MensLine Australia
Emotional health and relationship concerns for men:
www.mensline.org.au

QLife
LGBTIQ+ peer support: www.qlife.org.au

Rape & Domestic Violence Services Australia:
Support for survivors of sexual assault and domestic abuse:
www.rape-dvservices.org.au

ReachOut.com
Mental health for young people and their parents:
www.reachout.com

STARTTS
*NSW Service for the Treatment and Rehabilitation of Torture and
Trauma Survivors:* www.startts.org.au

Support Act
*Counselling for people working in Australian music or the
performing arts:* www.supportact.org.au

INDEX